A POWER
OF YOUR
OWN

A POWER OF YOUR OWN

HOW TO IGNITE YOUR POTENTIAL,
UNCOVER YOUR PURPOSE,
AND BLAZE YOUR OWN TRAIL
IN LIFE AND BUSINESS

NIKKI GROOM

NEW DEGREE PRESS

COPYRIGHT © 2020 NIKKI GROOM

All rights reserved.

A POWER OF YOUR OWN

How to Ignite Your Potential, Uncover Your Purpose, and Blaze Your Own Trail in Life and Business

ISBN   978-1-64137-995-3   *Paperback*

           978-1-64137-895-6   *Kindle Ebook*

           978-1-64137-896-3   *Ebook*

CONTENTS

———

INTRODUCTION

———

It's a hot August afternoon, and I'm leading a workshop entitled *How to Build Your Business from the Inside Out* in the heart of the Colorado Mountains.

Over the brow of the hill where we stand, you can peer down and see the campsite we're staying at. Behind us is the mouth of a labyrinth with small rocks bordering a single, continuous dirt path that winds its way slowly inward.

I ask everyone assembled to follow me as I lead them in a meandering spiral toward its center, and I begin to share my story.

I tell them what it was like launching my first business as a freelance copywriter and self-taught entrepreneur after a ten-year marketing career on either side of the Atlantic—first in the UK and then in the US. I admit to them that, in those early days, I didn't have a true sense of who I was or what I wanted. And so I looked to other people for answers.

Becoming a copywriter was someone else's idea. My business model was someone else's idea. The amount I charged for my services was someone else's idea. And while, on the outside, it looked like I had it made—I was booking out for months at a time and receiving referrals from people I didn't know—I doubted myself constantly and grappled with feeling like a fraud who had no right to be running a business.

I'd hoped doing my own thing would feel freeing, but instead, I felt trapped. I was earning more gross income than I ever had as an employee, but I felt like a prisoner of my own success.

I was doing everything on my own, I was swimming in deadlines, and I was unable to find space to work on my business so I could figure out how to earn more and scale. I felt overwhelmed, isolated, and frustrated. I was sacrificing my evenings and weekends to get things done, and I couldn't see how to make things work.

All the accolades, referrals, and dream clients in the world couldn't cover up the fact that I had created a business that worked for everyone else except myself.

Underneath the hot sun on this August afternoon with the benefit of hindsight, I understand that I had succumbed to the lies that the world had taught me to believe about myself: that I wasn't enough, and that I didn't deserve success or happiness. No wonder building a business felt to me like empty, exhausting work that wasn't sustainable in the long term. I was running my business from a disempowered place.

As we reach the center of the labyrinth, I turn to face the group and ask them about their deepest selves. I invite them to consider the ways in which they have allowed other people to influence what they feel, think, and do. And I have them consider what it would mean to relinquish the expectations of others in order to unleash their fullest potential and deepen their impact.

We make a decision, in that moment, to leave any beliefs in the heart of the labyrinth that no longer serve us as we explore how it might look if we allowed ourselves to lead from a more empowered place *all* the time; a place where our capacity for greatness is never in question.

As we circle back around toward the outer perimeter, I share the founding principles I used to rebuild my business from the inside out. I tell them about my journey to release the social conditioning that had been making me think, feel, and behave in self-sabotaging ways. And I reveal how I began to question any limiting beliefs that I had unconsciously accepted as truth.

In order to move forward, I had to go back—before the world had taught me what I could or couldn't do, and who I could or couldn't be. I had to remember that true personal power is generated from within and that brilliance was my birthright. Not only was I enough, but I had *always* been enough.

I tell them about the clients who became my teachers—and the storytellers who became my guides. I share how I learned that, **in a world in which so many of us are taught we don't belong, declaring, "I am in this world for a reason" is an act**

of resistance. I talk about how I learned to overcome perfectionism after discovering that no one has everything figured out—even when it may appear that way. And I emphasize the profound importance of living your life on purpose by tapping into your WHY and deepening into the work that's calling you forward.

Finally, I share how, instead of downplaying my talents and skills, I began using them more creatively in low-touch, high-impact ways to work with clients that helped me generate more than five figures a month for the first time in my life. As a strategist and consultant, I found I no longer had to trade my time for money or work long hours for a comparatively small paycheck like I had when I was a freelancer. People were hiring me for my expertise, and I was able to bring on other team members to manage different tasks and help me shave hours off my work week.

I discovered that being in business for yourself doesn't mean you have to sacrifice your well-being or what matters most to you. Neither do you have to choose between having an impact or making money, or sink into overwhelm because you're struggling to figure things out on your own.

You can make a real difference in the lives of others and give yourself a raise. You can own your power, stay rooted in the truth of who you are, and double your bottom line. And you can be of service to others and experience what it means to truly thrive.

Over a few years, I moved from copywriting to consulting to coaching before creating a business mentoring group for women business owners called the Movement Makers Mastermind—created to help women entrepreneurs tap into their inner power and purpose and step up as leaders.[1]

During each call, I hold space for participants to explore the work that lights them up as I reflect back to them the possibilities for their life and business. It's powerful work and the results speak for themselves—participants have been able to double their revenue during our time together.

By aligning my work with my experiences, values, and strengths, I've been able to uncover scalable and sustainable ways to drive positive impact. And today, I'm running a business that brings me joy, gives me purpose, and acts as a vehicle for me to disrupt the status quo by empowering other women to show up fully and lead with integrity.

The founding principles that helped me rebuild my business from the inside out are the same principles that I share in this book. And while you won't find a cookie-cutter guide to success in the pages that follow, I *do* share practical ways you can begin to uncover an intrinsic sense of potential and purpose—no matter whether you run a business now, choose to run a business in the future, or simply want to carve a more meaningful path through your career and life.

I wrote this book primarily for women business owners, but if you don't identify as a business owner or you don't identify as a woman, you will still benefit from the overarching

---

1   Nikki Groom, Movement Makers Mastermind, NikkiGroom.com, accessed July 6, 2020.

message. The world has taught so many of us to mistakenly believe that we're less than because of the simple fact of our race, ethnicity, gender, gender identity, sexual orientation, ability, socioeconomic status, and so on. My hope with this book is that it will act as a reminder of how incredible and powerful and capable you truly are, so that you will know—deep down—that you are enough, and you have the power to blaze a trail of your own.

If you're ready to embrace the truth of who you are, this book will reflect back to you the possibilities and remind you—over and over again—that you matter, your life matters, and you are needed on this planet.

Because **in these uncertain and chaotic times, it's your voice that we want, your message that we need, and your leadership that has the power to make a difference.**

PREFACE

———

It can be so easy to assume that we have all the time in the world. That we'll live our lives right through to 105 and, by some stroke of magic, get a chance to start all over again. But the truth is, time is slipping through our fingers with every passing second.

I've watched almost forty years of my life slip by, unannounced. And although I do not want to negate for even a second all the things I've learned and accomplished or all the ways I've grown, I also know that there's a big part of me that has been holding back, waiting to be told that it's my time to enter the ring.

But something I'm beginning to understand is that it has *always* been my time.

Yours too.

Many years ago, I decided to enter a real-life ring.

It was my first (and only) full-contact Muay Thai fight and, despite many years of training, nothing could have prepared me for what it felt like to have punches rain down on me in those first few seconds. With my back up against the ropes in a gymnasium full of people, I couldn't help but ask myself, *Was this a terrible mistake?*

But somehow, I found my feet and remembered my training. I began to land as many punches as I took. And, by the time the bell rang to announce the end of the second round, the odds were tipping in my favor. My six-days-a-week regimen had begun paying off while my opponent was getting tired. Her hands kept falling out of their protective guard around her face and dropping to her waist.

My sensei, Jake, yanked out a wooden stool for me to sit on before the bell rang for the final round. Wrapping a rough towel around my neck and squirting welcome relief into my mouth from the spout of a water bottle, he told me something that has stuck with me ever since.

"Nikki, *no one* can win this fight except YOU."

I immediately understood what he meant.

I could *feel* I was holding back out there. For every right hook I let fly, I'd hesitate afterward as if I was waiting for someone to tell me what to do next.

When the bell rang, Jake disappeared along with my stool, leaving me and my opponent sizing each other up from our respective corners of the ring. We approached each other tentatively—edging in, edging out—and then I seized my opportunity:

Jab-jab-CROSS!

With the cross, my opponent's eyes rolled back into her head and she staggered backward. The whole place leapt to its feet, whooping and hollering.

The referee took my opponent to one side and asked her if she was okay to continue. I watched her nod her head yes. But, when the final bell tolled, it was my hand the referee held high.

I never expected to win, but somehow I had.

I may be more of a yoga gal these days, but I've never forgotten Jake's words to me before that final round:

"*No one* can win this fight except YOU."

The way I was holding myself back in the ring is the way so many of us hold ourselves back in life and business. And in a world of deep structural unfairness, it's no wonder that we do! Why try when the odds are stacked against us? But when we recognize that we are, in fact, NOT the problem but the solution, we can begin to believe in ourselves once more.

You have the power to make an impact—even if you don't quite see that yet.

And in the pages that follow, I'll do my utmost to help you uncover that for yourself so that you can get *back* in that ring and give this thing called life everything you've got.

No permission needed.

1.

BUILDING YOUR PERSONAL POWER

1.

BRILLIANCE IS YOUR BIRTHRIGHT

---

*Can you remember who you were, before
the world told you who you should be?*

—CHARLES BUKOWSKI

Over almost ten years of coaching, strategizing with, and
supporting countless women entrepreneurs to live into their
highest potential, I've learned that acknowledging and owning your personal power—which is to say, your ability to
impact the world around you—is one of the most effective
ways to ignite your potential and blaze your own trail in life
and business.

The best part?

This type of power doesn't need to be gifted to you by anyone
else, because you can generate it from within—which means
everyone can be powerful.

Being the most powerful version of yourself is positive and life-affirming.[2] It gives you energy to forge ahead and live on purpose, no matter what life throws your way.

When you own your power, you're no longer a victim of circumstances. Instead, you turn challenges into opportunities. What other people think or say or do no longer fazes you. You stand up for your worth. You are certain about your potential. You believe in yourself and in what you can do. You take calculated risks outside your comfort zone. You demonstrate strength while admitting when you're wrong. You celebrate your accomplishments, and you don't take failure personally.

Power-from-within is not about dominating, controlling, or oppressing other people, which is how we traditionally think about power.[3] Neither is there a limited amount to go around. Instead, power-from-within is limitless, and you get to keep your power at the same time as you elevate others.[4]

There are several warning signs that you might not be fully owning your power. I share the following list not to make you feel badly about yourself, but to shine light on some of the ways in which society has taught women, in particular, that we don't deserve to have a voice and we don't deserve to have power. If you've found yourself falling into any of these behaviors in the past, I want you to know that not only is it entirely understandable, but it's also not your fault.

---

2   Amy Allen, "Feminist Perspectives on Power," *The Stanford Encyclopedia of Philosophy*, Fall 2016 edition.

3   Ibid.

4   Ibid.

While this list isn't exhaustive, my hope is that it will help you bring more awareness to the areas in your life or business where you've been feeling disempowered or getting in your own way.

SIX SIGNS OF DISEMPOWERMENT

1. You find it hard to say no or express what you want.
2. You don't set healthy boundaries that teach people how to treat you.
3. You're overdependent on the opinions of others.
4. You second guess yourself and worry about making mistakes.
5. You don't pursue your dreams because you assume you don't have what it takes.
6. You sabotage your success with habits that allow you to sidestep your potential.

In business, this might look like you discounting your services simply because someone asks you to, giving in to scope creep, not marketing yourself because you're worried about what people might think, overcommitting to too many projects at once, procrastinating, focusing on busywork, thinking you have to do everything yourself, or failing to start or complete projects that would move you closer to your goals.

In life, this might look like saying yes every time someone asks you to do them a favor—even if you don't have the bandwidth, allowing someone else to make decisions on your behalf, beating yourself up whenever you mess up, or burying your head in the sand rather than taking care of something that's important to you because it's easier to avoid it completely.

It can take a lot of mental determination to step out of a disempowered mindset, but it's never too late to own your power.

In the Movement Makers Mastermind, a business growth accelerator I run each year to support women entrepreneurs to amplify their impact and their income, we meet each quarter to plan out the following twelve weeks. At the beginning of each planning session, I have everyone write down a five-year vision for their businesses that's "unobstructed by their current reality"—meaning it shouldn't be restricted by their current mindset, schedule, energy levels, team, skills, or resources. Afterward, I have them speak their vision into existence as if it were true today and, one by one, I get to witness each person revel in the possibilities for their lives. They shift out of fear and into faith. They begin to give themselves permission to dream a little bigger and reach a little higher.

Inevitably though, when we move into the next phase of our quarterly planning sessions—which is when each entrepreneur begins to map out what she needs to do in the more immediate future to move her businesses closer to that vision—doubts begin to crowd in. Excuses surface. Fear reasserts itself. And for a moment, the vision they created just moments before is in real danger of evaporating into thin air.

I help them mitigate this fight-or-flight response by asking them the following questions and encouraging them to face their fears head on:

- What might get in the way of you accomplishing these goals?
- Whose support do you need to enlist to help you accomplish these goals?
- What do you need to learn in order to accomplish these goals?
- What experiments do you need to run in order to accomplish these goals?
- What will you have to start doing differently in order to accomplish these goals?

Answering these questions helps prepare them for success with an objective assessment of what's actually possible.

SETTLING FOR LESS THAN WE DESERVE

As we get older, many of us start to put words before our dreams. We pad our sentences to excuse our inaction and remove any fear or pressure or urgency. We say:

"I'm thinking about…"

"I might try to…"

"One day, I will…"

Thinking. Trying. One day.

We buffer the fear and give ourselves space to do nothing. We protect ourselves against uncertainty and the potential for failure. And at the same time, we unconsciously push our purpose out of plain sight and then later wonder how we managed to lose ourselves so completely.

If you'd asked me when I was a child what I wanted to be when I grew up, I would have responded without hesitation, "I want to be a writer." Just like that. My ambition was as plain and simple and true as that sentence. No question about it. No concerns about how I'd get there. It was just a fact—one no one would dare argue with me about.

I didn't realize how hard it can be to break into publishing, or that it would be almost four decades before I'd finally get around to writing my first book (the one you're reading)—never mind everything that would happen and I would accomplish in between.

I was too young to understand that life can sometimes be *hard*, and confusing, and mess with your head and your self-esteem. I didn't recognize how much so many of us are forced to constantly absorb the message throughout our lives that we are less than, that we don't belong, or that we aren't enough. And I didn't realize how much these outside messages would gradually erode my self-image and convince me the world was oblivious to my happiness and perhaps even pitted against it.

I admire that younger version of myself—the gutsy, determined little girl who simply assumed her life was destined for greatness before she was sucked into a maelstrom of insecurities too believable to shake. Sadly, this slide into self-doubt is endemic among young girls.

"Girls' self-esteem peaks when they are nine years old, then takes a nose dive," says clinical psychologist Robin F. Goodman.[5] Not only that, but seven out of every ten girls believe they aren't good enough or don't measure up in some way because they perceive themselves to be inadequate, unlovable, or incompetent. Once formed, this sense of not measuring up permeates every thought, producing faulty assumptions and ongoing self-defeating behavior.[6]

- Over 70 percent of girls age fifteen to seventeen avoid normal daily activities, such as attending school, when they feel bad about their looks.[7]

- Seventy-five percent of girls with low self-esteem report engaging in negative activities like cutting, bullying, smoking, drinking, or disordered eating.[8]

- By age thirteen, 53 percent of American girls age thirteen are "unhappy with their bodies." This grows to 78 percent by the time girls reach seventeen.[9]

5   Natalia Brzezinski, "Building Our Daughters' Self Esteem, by Starting with Our Own," *HuffPost*, updated November 2011.

6   Fredric Neuman, MD, "Low Self-Esteem," *Psychology Today*, posted April 2013.

7   "Brands in Action: Dove," Unilever USA, accessed July 10, 2020.

8   "11 Facts About Teens and Self-Esteem," *Do Something*, accessed July 10, 2020.

9   "Get The Facts," National Organization for Women, accessed July 10, 2020.

When I hear these statistics, I'm grateful for the work my client Lisa Van Ahn, a professional kickboxer and founder of the I AM Initiative, does. Lisa created the I AM Initiative to teach young girls the power of their thoughts, the difference between intuition and fear, the importance of self-love, and what it means to live positively and responsibly using their inner superpowers.[10]

At nineteen years old, an abusive boyfriend pushed Lisa out of his Bronco after a volatile argument and she landed on the curb of a kickboxing studio. She walked up to the entrance and decided to go inside and try a class. That decision changed the course of her entire life. After putting on some gloves and punching some pads, Lisa immediately felt stronger and more confident. That was the day she decided to stop feeling like a victim and start moving down the path of confidence and self-love.[11]

She kept returning to train every day and, gradually, her self-esteem rocketed. The two sisters who owned the studio encouraged and supported her, and it was the first time Lisa had ever felt seen in her whole life. She explains, "They could see my strength and power, even when I couldn't see it myself."

After a year or so, Lisa decided she wanted to fight in competitions. She won her first fight and realized she had never felt so sure of herself or proud of what she could do. Martial arts enabled her to start releasing the trauma and false beliefs that

---

10   Lisa Van Ahn, "About I Am Girl," I Am Initiative, accessed July 9, 2020.

11   Ellen Fondiler, "An Interview with Lisa Van Ahn," *Unlocked,* accessed June 24, 2020.

had haunted her for most of her life and she went on to kick-box at the Pan-Am games in Brazil, winning a bronze medal.

"When we believe we're unworthy, there isn't a defense system in the world that will protect us," Lisa shares. "I know this is true because I experienced it. I grew up believing in the negative things that others were saying about me and I let it shut me down. My self-doubt stole my ability to see the brilliance that was my birthright."[12]

It took me a long time to realize that brilliance was my birthright too. And even though I kept striving in that general direction—I worked hard at school and didn't give my parents much trouble—another emerging belief had begun to take hold: that I wasn't enough, that I would never *be* enough, and I would always have to settle for whatever scraps life decided to throw my way.

That belief has been responsible for so many times in my life when I have held myself back, said yes too quickly, stayed too long, and settled for less: less money, less love, less peace, less freedom, less happiness.

Many of us settle for a life that's smaller than our dreams despite having so much more to give.

Minda Harts, bestselling author of *The Memo: What Women of Color Need to Know to Secure a Seat at the Table*, shares, "As a child, the adult figures in my life always told me the

---

12   Lisa Van Ahn, "About Lisa Van Ahn," I Am Initiative, accessed July 9, 2020.

'sky's the limit,' or 'reach for the stars.' I would stretch out my short arms and tiny hands above my head as I looked up and thought about my future. In times that I faced adversity, I would think about those phrases I often heard and remembered how I felt when I thought about my possibilities. Gender and race never crossed my mind as I reached for what was mine. The world was my oyster, and it was up for a fair game if you dared to try."[13]

But when she entered adulthood, those phrases no longer meant the same to her. "Now there was a glass ceiling that stood in my way from reaching any stars." She adds, "The glass ceiling is thicker for African-American women."[14]

You're more likely to live beneath your potential if you've been conditioned by society to view barriers to your success as insurmountable obstacles.

In a world in which leadership is regarded as the preserve of straight cis-gender able-bodied white men, white supremacist and patriarchal cultures may well have persuaded you that:

- There is only one "right way" to do things.
- Making a mistake is the same as *being* a mistake.
- Needing help indicates weakness, and you're only valuable if you can get things done on your own without guidance.

---

13   Minda Harts, "Glass Ceilings Aren't Created Equal: Confronting the Barriers Black Women Face in the Workplace," *LinkedIn,* published on September 13, 2019.

14   Ibid.

- Decision making should be left to those with more power, whether or not they have empathy for our viewpoint or experience.

The first step to dismantling these cultural assumptions is to work to shift your mindset, noticing any negative narratives that rise to the surface, recognizing that they didn't originate from you, and reframing them.[15] I'll share some more about how you can do that in the coming chapters.

Here, in your hands, is proof that I knew better at seven years old what I was capable of than I did at seventeen or twenty-seven or even thirty-seven years old. But while my seven-year-old self unthinkingly applied for a publishing deal with Penguin Books (I kid you not—they sent me a very kind rejection letter), I had to go through months of grueling self-doubt before I came anywhere close to writing this first chapter.

It makes me wonder, what if—instead of fixating on what the world tells us we can or can't do or can or can't be—we trusted our big and brave and beautiful hearts to lead us in the right direction? What dreams might we reclaim if we chose to believe a different story?

USE THESE POWER PROMPTS
Where haven't you been fully owning your power?

---

15   For a full list, see Kenneth Jones and Tema Okun, "The Characteristics of White Supremacy Culture," *Dismantling Racism: A Workbook for Social Change Groups*, ChangeWork, 2001.

How might you live your life differently and on your own terms if you owned your power from within every day?

STEAL THIS POWER STATEMENT

I own my power and believe in the future I'm creating for myself.

———————————————————————

2.

YOU ARE WILDLY CAPABLE

———

Self-doubt is proof of your humanity,
not your inadequacy.

—TANYA GEISLER

As Leanne typed her information into the application form for the Movement Makers Mastermind, she felt a swell of despair sweep over her. Sighing heavily, she lifted her gaze out of the window of her home office and watched as the trees shook crisp orange leaves off weary branches.

Filling out this application felt like a make-or-break moment for her. For the past year, she had been feeling increasingly disillusioned about her web design business and uncertain whether it made sense to keep the doors open. She was tired of asking herself, *Am I cut out for this?* and wished someone could simply deliver the answer to her in an envelope so she didn't have to wonder anymore.

It wasn't that she didn't have any clients, or plenty of them, and it wasn't that she didn't have years of experience—this year marked her sixth in business for herself—but she still didn't *feel* like a "real" businesswoman.

Worrying constantly about where her next client would come from, she overcommitted to too many projects at once to keep uncertainty at bay. And, while she had plenty of ideas for how she wanted to grow her business, she was always too busy to get those ideas out of her head and into the world.

Every night, she tossed and turned, feeling too anxious to fall asleep. And every morning, she woke up with a knot in her stomach.

She couldn't continue like this.

Something had to give.

* * *

When I received Leanne's application, her answer to the question, "Why do you want to join this mastermind?" grabbed me by the heartstrings.

She had replied, *I'm trying to extricate myself from the lie that what I have to offer isn't that special or valuable.*

How many of us have felt that way—whether we're working for ourselves or somebody else or nobody else?

I have personally wrestled for years with the belief that what I have to offer isn't special or valuable. And I now understand that this belief is a lie.

You, too, have something special and valuable to offer the world. And, when you catch yourself questioning your worthiness, reminding yourself of everything you've overcome to get where you are today can be a powerful exercise in conquering self-doubt.

Don't believe me? Look back at your life and allow yourself a moment to celebrate all the major milestones you've left in your wake.

It could be anything that meant something to you: The time you quit college to follow your heart. The time you ditched the person who treated you terribly. The time you stood your ground at work. The time you moved across the country for your dream job. The time you found your first paying client. The first time you fired a client. The time you protested about a cause you believed in. The time you singlehandedly homeschooled two children and held down a business while a pandemic raged outside your window. Every accomplishment. Every hard knock. All of it.

You might want to grab a journal and jot down a list and keep it handy. Or you might find a quiet moment to sit with your spine straight, feet grounded on the floor, eyes closed as you contemplate one milestone after another.

* * *

After Leanne joined the Movement Makers Mastermind, it became rapidly apparent just how gifted she really was. Not only did she take genuine pleasure in achieving high standards of excellence in the delivery of her design projects, but she was also deeply committed to the relationships she formed with her clients along the way. She actually *cared* about the people she worked with, and she wanted what was in their best interests. She had a unique way of looking at the problems they needed solving. And in turn, she had positioned herself as an irreplaceable resource. She just couldn't clearly *see* that yet.

On our calls, her fellow Mastermind members and I encouraged her to voice her doubts and fears out loud. And week after week, we reflected back to her the *true* story: that she was not only capable but *wildly* capable. That she was exceptionally talented and intuitive and wise. And that she brought so much more to the table than she had ever allowed herself to recognize.

Over the next several months, Leanne became unrecognizable as the struggling business owner who didn't believe in herself and didn't *feel* like a CEO. Her confidence rose exponentially. She recruited a new team member who turned out to be a remarkable fit. She reworked her business model. And, to her surprise, she doubled her revenue.

But while Leanne was proactively taking action to grow her business, the *real* change happened before she had taken a single step, when she began seeing herself as the woman she is: talented, accomplished, and worthy of a fulfilling business and a life on purpose.

We tend to keep any lack of self-esteem under wraps because we're afraid other people will judge us harshly. But there is power in admitting our self-doubt out loud and in safe spaces where we know we will be held and heard and supported.

Leanne did exactly that when she joined the Mastermind and surrounded herself with women who were only too happy to reassure her that she was on the right track and *did* have what it took to succeed.

By being willing to vulnerably express her challenges to her peers, Leanne was able to surface the stories she had been telling herself—that she wasn't cut out for entrepreneurship and that she had nothing valuable to offer—and ultimately, free herself from the limiting beliefs that had been holding her back from embracing her full potential.

Not only that but hearing how Leanne was struggling encouraged the other women in the group to admit they had been doubting themselves in similar ways.

This is the power of exposing your rough edges to people you trust. It not only helps you regain your sense of self, but it also helps others see themselves in your stories and feel less alone in their struggles.

THE IMPOSTER COMPLEX

The term *Imposter Phenomenon* (also known as the *Imposter Complex*, the *Imposter Experience*, and the *Imposter Syndrome*—although it's not actually a clinical diagnosis) was first coined by clinical psychologists Pauline Rose Clance and Suzanne Ament Imes in their groundbreaking 1978 research study, *The Imposter Phenomenon in High Achieving Women: Dynamics and Therapeutic Intervention.*[16]

In the study, Clance and Imes interviewed 150 high-functioning, high-performing women and noticed a common pattern: the women seemed incapable of internalizing their successes. Instead, they often felt incompetent or believed their accomplishments had come about not through genuine ability but as a result of having been lucky, having worked harder than others, or having deceived someone into thinking they were smart and capable. In contrast, they could easily internalize their failures.

While Clance and Imes identified this pattern in women, subsequent studies have revealed the *Imposter Complex* does not discriminate based on gender. In other words, no matter how you identify, if you are high-functioning and high-achieving, there's a more than 70 percent chance that you will experience the Imposter Complex at some point.[17]

---

16 Joe Langford and Pauline Rose Clance, "The Imposter Phenomenon: Recent Research Findings Regarding Dynamics, Personality and Family Patterns and Their Implications for Treatment," *Psychotherapy* 30, no. 3, Fall 1993.

17 Olivia Goldhill, "Is Imposter Syndrome a Sign of Greatness?" *QZ*, accessed on June 18, 2020.

When leadership coach Tanya Geisler first stumbled across Clance and Imes's findings, she felt relieved. She had been working for years in what was an outwardly successful, but ultimately unsatisfying, career in advertising. And, while she kept waiting for deep-seated feelings of accomplishment and satisfaction to arrive, they never did. Instead, she continued to suffer from a myriad of "not good enough, not smart enough, not ready enough" beliefs and worried that it was just a matter of time before her career crumbled beneath her.

"Any success I enjoyed I chalked up to someone else having made a mistake," she shares. "I thought it was just a matter of time before they found out I was a fake."[18]

Discovering that she had been experiencing the Imposter Complex and there was nothing inherently unworthy about her led Tanya to feel freer than she had in years. "I discovered that the more successful you are, the more likely you are to feel like you don't deserve your success, which, quite frankly, means that most of us are in excellent company."

Not only are you in excellent company, but the Imposter Complex is not your fault to begin with.

In a broken society that profits from our self-doubt, we have been programmed to believe that if we don't fit a certain mold, we don't measure up.

When Nicola Andrews attended three separate training sessions about the Imposter Complex during her first six

---

18   Tanya Geisler, "About," TanyaGeisler.com, accessed on June 18, 2020.

months as a librarian for the University of San Francisco, she noticed that the onus was on her to "get over" any feelings of inferiority. But as a Māori, takatāpui immigrant, person of color, and first-generation scholar, Nicola knew that feeling like an imposter was the direct result of systems of colonization, white supremacy, misogyny, and hatred that continue to operate within our society. "The lack of belonging I felt did not stem from a lack of self-esteem," she wrote, "but from the knowledge that libraries and academia as institutions *never intended* I belong."[19]

In other words, the Imposter Complex results from an imbalance of power that shouldn't exist in the first place. It's a patriarchal wound that relies on white, heterosexual, able-bodied, cis-gendered men remaining on the top of society and leaving little room for anyone else.

Recognizing where you need to shift your mindset is always powerful and effective.

AND...

It's important to recognize that your self-doubt is rooted in systems and structures that were not built for you, and yet impact you nonetheless.

Business mentor Jo Casey writes that our culture is giving us messages *all the time* about the rules women are expected to

---

19   Nicola Andrews, "It's Not Imposter Syndrome: Resisting Self-Doubt as Normal for Library Workers," *In the Library with the Lead Pipe, An Open Access Peer Reviewed Journal*, accessed on June 18, 2020.

follow. We're expected to be "small, thin, softly spoken, pretty and sexy—but not sexual and definitely not slutty, giving (to the point of putting themselves last), compliant, agreeable, non-confrontational, private, polite, nurturing, perfect... and certainly not the most brilliant one in the room."

She continued, "Sometimes [these messages are] so subtle we only notice [them] when we violate those rules. OR we are approaching violating them—that's when our own internal protective system kicks in and creates resistance around the 'dangerous' action."[20]

Here are just three of those internal protective systems to look out for, which you may have been conditioned to work from:

1. **Perfectionism.** Working three times as hard as your peers to make sure they don't find out that you're a "fraud." Procrastinating and not taking action in case you experience failure. And regularly focusing on what's not working rather than what is.

2. **People pleasing.** Going out of your way to ensure people like you. Never saying no and always trying to do too much instead of what's realistic. Having unhealthy boundaries that involve disregarding your values, desires, needs, and limits.

3. **Diminishment**. Dimming your light so that other people feel comfortable.[21] Allowing your critical inner voice

---

20   Jo Casey, "Feminine Conditioning," JoCasey.com, accessed on June 18, 2020.

21   Tanya Geisler, "Diminishment and the Imposter Complex," TanyaGeisler.com, accessed on June 25, 2020.

to take charge. Negatively comparing yourself to others and measuring your value based on what other people are doing.

If you want to override these coping mechanisms, the first step is not to blame yourself but also not to deny that this conditioning is happening if you want to stop doubting your potential.

Here are some workarounds to help you break the hold the Imposter Complex has over you:

FIVE IMPOSTER COMPLEX WORKAROUNDS

1. **Visualize your success.** Create a vision of the future that you want to transform into reality. Picture your success. Speak your vision into existence as if it were true today, like the masterminders did in the last chapter. Making the effort to map out a strategic plan of action will help you feel better equipped to handle whatever comes your way.

2. **Be objective.** Instead of taking the limiting beliefs the Imposter Complex surfaces to heart, notice the systems, processes, and approaches you've developed that allow you to do your best work. Separate yourself from the work that you do by being objective about the outcomes you can generate.

3. **Gather proof.** Make a list that proves you're qualified to do the work that you do. You can refer to this list whenever you need a confidence boost. Create a success log and record every big win and tiny victory. If your clients send

you glowing praise or positive feedback, save the emails to a specific email folder, or pin their thank you cards or notes to a cork board on the wall above your desk. Frame any notable press mentions. Read the testimonials or endorsements people have written about you and your work.

4. **Meditate.** Some apps, like Insight Timer, have guided meditations specifically geared toward overcoming the Imposter Complex. These can help you bring awareness to the lies that the Imposter Complex has told you about yourself. With regular practice, you'll find you can tune into a deep inner knowing, which is your consciousness, and which remains unchanged and unhindered by any of the limiting stories you hear in your mind about yourself.

5. **Surround yourself with the right people.** Seek role models who show you what's possible without making you feel less than. Instead of looking for inspiration from the top 1 percent—for example, the person who has hundreds of thousands of followers on Instagram—notice who among your peers is a few steps ahead of you. What can you learn from them? Instead of isolating yourself, consider creating or joining a mastermind group with people who understand the challenges you're up against, and who can encourage you and give you the feedback you need to push forward.

🎧 **PODCAST TIP**

Listen to my interview with leadership coach Tanya Geisler as we discuss the Imposter Complex on the Movement Makers podcast.

Visit nikkigroom.com/category/podcast/.[22]

READY ENOUGH

One of the lies the Imposter Complex teaches us to believe about ourselves is, "I'm not ready yet." After I launched my first business as a copywriter for women entrepreneurs in 2012, I genuinely believed I had to work harder and harder to *feel* ready so I could go after what I wanted: whether it was scoring a certain client, writing an article for a renowned media outlet, or creating a new product, program, or course.

For years, I'd been listening to Srinivas Rao interview guests from all walks of life on his podcast, *The Unmistakable Creative*. Srini has interviewed several hundred of the world's most interesting people—from bank robbers, drug dealers, and billionaires to many of my peers and people I look up to and admire. For a long time I told myself that when I *felt* ready enough, I would pitch myself to be a guest on his show.

Only after I stumbled across an article online about self-sabotaging beliefs did I realize *I'm not ready yet* was actually code for *I'm scared, I don't feel worthy, and I'm worried what other people will think.*

I didn't have to wait until I felt 100 percent ready—and neither do you.

You can decide you're ready enough now and act accordingly.

---

22   Nikki Groom, "Tanya Geisler: Stepping Into Your Starring Role," NikkiGroom.com, accessed on July 8, 2020.

You can summon enough courage to start where you are with what you have and figure things out as you go. You can grab hold of opportunities with both hands and afterward figure out how to make the best of them. You can trust your intuition and wade into the unknown, not needing all the answers in order to take action.

Armed with my new understanding of self-sabotaging beliefs, I began telling myself, *I'm ready now,* whenever the lie popped up in my mind.

When Srini reached out to me about a book he was writing that he wanted my help promoting, I took the plunge and asked him to consider having me as his guest on *The Unmistakable Creative.* "I've always wanted to ask you," I wrote, "but would tell myself, *I'm not ready yet.* Well, I'm ready now."

Srini agreed to my request right away, and I realized that, by catching the self-sabotaging lie and reframing it, I had freed myself up to live into a more empowered reality.

In the book *The Confidence Code: The Science and Art of Self-Assurance—What Women Should Know,* journalists Katty Kay and Claire Shipman interview women leaders from the worlds of politics, sports, the military, and the arts and, ultimately, argue that confidence is not a fixed psychological state.[23] Instead, it requires a choice: it asks that we worry

---

23   Katty Kay and Claire Shipman, *The Confidence Code: The Science and Art of Self-Assurance: What Women Should Know,* Harper Business, first edition, April 15, 2014.

less about pleasing others or being perfect, and more about taking action, taking risks, and failing forward.

I thought I had to put my hopes and dreams and desires on the shelf until some arbitrary moment in the future. I didn't understand that we are *all* works in progress—and we always will be. No one has it all figured out. We are *always* evolving and changing and improving and growing more fully into ourselves.

And, if we wait until we *feel* ready, we'll be waiting a long, long time.

USE THESE POWER PROMPTS
Where has the Imposter Complex been holding you back in your life?

What could shift in your life or business if you said, "I'm ready now"?

STEAL THIS POWER STATEMENT
I'm ready now to live the life I've always wanted.

3.

YOU HAVE ALWAYS BEEN WORTHY

———

Your worth is far beyond what you know.

—M. J. KOCOVSKI

Grace Quantock was sure she wasn't the first student to lie dazedly on the floor, words slurring, world spinning, struggling to stand. But in her case, it wasn't Friday night at the Student Union bar. She was lying on the sixth-floor landing in the Humanities building trying to get to her history seminar. And she wasn't drunk but disabled. As she lay there, looking up, watching her peers walk past her to class, she wondered how on earth she had ended up in that position.

"There are few things more devastating to a young girl on the cusp of making her mark on the world than having her dreams wrenched away. I was that girl," Grace explained to a rapt audience from her wheelchair on the stage at TEDx Aylesbury after relaying this story. "Like so many others, I was *normal*—I had hopes and dreams—and then, suddenly, I wasn't."[24]

When doctors diagnosed Grace with a cocktail of life-changing auto-immune illnesses at the age of eighteen, she was swept up in a whirlwind of pain, struggle, diagnoses, and confusion. "I felt that even showing up to life was impossible in my state."

Grace felt her otherness the most when planning a simple shopping trip. Even getting out of bed, getting dressed, and making a shopping list was challenging because of her painful aches and joints, memory loss, and cognitive dysfunction.

At the bus stop, people stared at her. "I'd be forced to justify, defend, and explain my otherness."

"My dear, what's wrong with you?" people would ask.

"All I wanted was to go shopping just like them," Grace admitted. "All I wanted was to be normal. And I felt the only way to achieve normality was to not be ill anymore."

She spent hours online searching desperately for a miracle cure, but doctors said she was wasting her time and should go home and get used to living with her diagnoses. Except that it didn't really *feel* like living to Grace.

---

24   Grace Quantock, "Using Your "Brokenness" to Break Boundaries," TEDx Aylesbury, accessed on June 19, 2020.

Instead, she made up her mind to do everything in her power not to give up on herself, but to research ways to alleviate her symptoms and give her body the best possible chance of healing itself—such as eating an anti-inflammatory diet so she could take fewer anti-inflammatory painkillers.

After starting her new diet, she was talking to a friend one day in her kitchen when another friend popped his head around the door. He looked at the jar of bright green vegetable juice in her hand and exclaimed, "*Grace!* That looks *disgusting!*"

All at once, Grace felt like a weirdo, a misfit, and a freak. "It hurt," she shared. Speaking to her husband Linus afterward, she cried, "I'm fed up with always being the sick chick and always being the weirdo."

"But Grace, what if you aren't?" Linus replied. "What if you aren't the misfit? What if you're the *pioneer?* What if you aren't the freak? What if you're the *trailblazer?*"

That moment changed everything for Grace. Deciding to no longer allow herself to be defined by anyone else's perception of her illnesses, she completed her degree in History with the support of Linus before taking six months off to figure out her next steps. That six months turned into three years, two businesses, and a global movement.

Today, Grace is an award-winning international wellness expert, coach, author, founder, and motivational speaker who is recognized as a trailblazer by thousands of people who have seen her speak and participated in her programs. But she doesn't want people to be under any mistaken beliefs about her journey.

"People want me to tell the Hero's Journey story," she told me, "but this story is not the girl in the wheelchair made good. Living well, and not a miracle cure story, is my happy ending. And this story isn't just about me; it applies to us all—wheelchair or not, illness or not—because we all are human, we all struggle, and we all carry wounds in our own ways. And this story is not about fitting in, because when you embrace your otherness, you can do so much more."[25]

You might be "othered" if you have relatively less power in society because of your race, gender, sexual orientation, ethnicity, socioeconomic status, ability, or sexual orientation, for example. As someone who is othered, you might find it easy to believe that you're less than because you don't share power with the dominant group, but nothing could be further from the truth. And when you embrace the reality of what you're capable of, you not only embrace your otherness, but you empower yourself to contribute to your fullest potential—in life and business.

EMBRACE LIBERATING TRUTHS
Our fears tend to express themselves most powerfully when we're pursuing things that really matter to us.

You might have noticed them creep in through below-the-surface doubts that make you second guess yourself on the

---

25   Ibid.

brink of a big decision or an important first step. Suddenly, you find yourself unable to ascertain whether you have all the information you need or are doing the right thing. Unable to choose and unable to act, you stay inside your comfort zone and watch as opportunities pass you by.

At times likes these, you're likely to hear a familiar voice. It's the voice of your inner critic, generated by those who have othered you—on a personal, cultural, or structural level—and which wants to prevent you from doing anything it deems you unqualified for. But studies have shown that women are much more qualified than they ever give themselves credit for.[26]

I was twenty-two when I secured my first "real" job as the marketing manager of the UK subsidiary of a global manufacturer and spent the next five years devoting myself to the company and transforming their marketing into something they could be proud of. But near the end of that time, I realized I was ready for a new challenge.

Around then, the marketing manager for the North American subsidiary handed in her two-weeks' notice. When she emailed her international colleagues to let us know what a pleasure it had been working with us, my heart skipped a beat. I wondered to myself, *Could I move to America and take over her job?*

---

26   Tara Sophia Mohr, "Why Women Don't Apply For Jobs Unless They're 100 Percent Qualified," *Harvard Business Review*, accessed July 6, 2020.

Almost immediately, my inner critic rushed in and set me straight: *Don't be stupid, Nikki! You can't live in AMERICA!*

But something in the universe had been set in motion, and within six months I was saying a teary goodbye to my parents at Heathrow Airport. I was twenty-seven years old and leaving everything and everyone I'd ever known. Two stuffed suitcases accompanied me to the airport, packed to the brim with my life for the foreseeable future.

Three thousand miles is a long way away from home. It's a long way from anywhere. But this opportunity was everything to me—my chance to leap, to plant roots somewhere new. So many people told me how brave I was, that they could never do what I had found the courage to do. But they didn't know that if I had listened to my inner critic, I would never have left.

Limiting self-beliefs that originate from your inner critic are often rooted in absolutes and sound like:

I can't _____

I'm not _____

I will never _____

These beliefs typically hide out in places where you're currently producing results you don't want.[27] That means they are often already silently sabotaging your success by

---

27   Matt James, PhD, "4 Steps to Release 'Limiting Beliefs' Learned from Childhood," *Psychology Today*, accessed June 19, 2020.

convincing you that you don't have what it takes to succeed. If you're not careful, they can inform the way you see the world and operate in it and prevent you from doing your best work.

One of the best ways I've found to manage these beliefs is to catch them as they float into my conscious mind and reframe them. Of course, no reframed belief will magically change anything overnight, but it does give me a jolt and a reminder not to internalize my oppression or stand in my own way.

I do this with each Mastermind group I run every time we begin a new quarter together. I ask each participant to think about and write down the limiting beliefs that have been holding them back, and then reframe those beliefs so they can live in a different reality.

In his book, *Your Best Year Ever*, Michael Hyatt describes limiting beliefs as "a misunderstanding of the present that shortchanges the future," and suggests that, instead of limiting beliefs, we embrace liberating truths.[28]

In other words, we can choose to be whoever we want to be.

You really can rewire your mind, recalibrate your outlook, and create a vision for change that's unobstructed by your current reality.

Being in business for myself has forced me to examine any feelings of unworthiness when they surface and meet them

---

28   Michael Hyatt, *Your Best Year Ever: A 5-Step Plan for Achieving Your Most Important Goals*, Baker Books, January 2018.

with compassion to get back to a place where I can believe in my potential and move forward unencumbered by negative thinking.

As I mentioned in the last chapter, one of my limiting beliefs has been *I'm not ready yet*, and now every time I catch that belief floating up to the surface, I grab it and reframe it to a liberating truth: *I'm ready now.*

The world is constantly telling us that we aren't enough: not pretty enough, not smart enough, not accomplished enough, not white enough, not thin enough, and the list goes on—and these stories are constantly being reinforced by what we read, what we watch, and what we witness play out in our social media feeds and on our television screens.

So when the whole world is pitched against us, who will tell us the truth about who we really are?

We *have* to do that for ourselves.

Because the truth is you *are* enough. You have *always* been enough. And you are capable of more than you ever imagined possible. And nothing and no one will ever change that fact.

CHOOSE WHO YOU WANT TO BE

I find that my darkest thoughts most often derail me when I'm living from my head and not my heart. But when I spend time in quiet meditation, I can often center myself in the truth of who I am. I realize that *I am enough, just the way I am.* I am fallible and imperfect, and that's normal and human and okay. My dreams aren't outside my grasp. They're just waiting for me to take action.

In these moments, something central is restored and I feel fully alive and inherently worthy. I finally feel powerful and hopeful and free. I am more aware than ever that—before the unjust systems of the world get a say—on a core level, I have limitless potential.

Whoever we think we are and whatever we believe our flaws to be are actually just projections influenced by a biased, discriminatory, and inequitable society. They aren't real. They don't represent our *true* selves. But somehow, we get attached to the idea that they are and they do. We think that because we feel anger, we must be an angry person. Or that because we feel fear, we must be too afraid to do the thing we wish, deep down, that we could do. As a result, shame crowds in and convinces us to play small. Stuck in place, we find ourselves unable to move forward.

But it *is* possible to let go of those thoughts and beliefs as soon as they appear. We really can rewire our brains to love ourselves first before we judge ourselves. We can remember that we are whatever and whoever we choose to be.

My close friend Bethany O, a talented photographer—or, as she says, "light catcher," who teaches people how to shine in front of the camera—once wrote about how, at any moment, her then-sixteen-month-old daughter was likely to throw her head back, laugh heartily at the sky, and run forward blindly with arms back and chest out until she collapsed to the ground in a fit of laughter. "It's one of the most beautiful things I've ever witnessed," Bethany wrote, "and it happens (seemingly) unprovoked."

It made her chew over her tagline for her photography business, "let it shine," to better understand how she could apply the idea of letting it shine *all* the time. "One thing that is very clear to me from watching my kids," she wrote, "is that 'Lettin' It Shine' is not something we need to *learn*. It's something we are *born* knowing. It's something that we (tragically) *unlearn* over time."[29]

The possibilities for my life have been constrained by the limits of my imagination and the stories I told myself. But I'm not my past mistakes, my worst traits, or my negative thoughts—and I can't be defined by those things either.

And neither can you.

TAKE ACTION
Make a list of all the limiting beliefs that have been holding you back. Can you flip them on their head and write a *new* list of liberating truths that assume the opposite is true?

You might want to ceremoniously burn your first list afterward or destroy it by tearing it into tiny shreds. Whatever feels good to you...

---

29   Bethany Pearson O'Connor, "Right on Time to Break the Cycle," *Huff-Post*, accessed June 19, 2020.

Take your new list and consider writing your favorites on sticky notes where you can see them each day—like on your bathroom mirror. Some jewelry and accessory companies like My Intent and MantraBand allow you to wear your truths as reminders. Or you might want to use a journal each morning like Intelligent Change's *The Five-Minute Journal*, which provides a dedicated space for you to record a daily affirmation.[30]

I'm also a huge fan of Sah D'Simone's abundance meditation, "Manifest Your Dreams," which you can access for free on the Insight Timer app.[31] This guided meditation will help you shift from a mindset of scarcity, which is fearful and anxious, to an abundance mindset, which is creative and full of possibilities.

There's no right or wrong way to do this. The idea is to simply expend *more* energy toward remembering how limitless you really are and *less* time focusing on the lies the world has persuaded you to believe about yourself.

Remember: You are worthy, and you have always been worthy.

Nothing and no one can change that fact.

---

30   "The Five-Minute Journal: A Happier You in 5 Minutes a Day," Intelligent Change (May 23, 2013)

31   Sah D'Simone, "Powerful Abundance Meditation—Manifest Your Dreams," Insight Timer, accessed on July 13, 2020.

THE IMPORTANCE OF PATIENT PRACTICE

Although it would be great to think we can simply eliminate any negative beliefs from our lives by repeating positive affirmations, shifting our self-identity isn't generally that easy or fast.

To *truly* believe what we're telling ourselves, we need to not only exercise patience but be prepared to practice reframing our beliefs and rewiring our brains every day—with the understanding that we might patiently be practicing for the rest of our lives.

Some time ago, I attended one of a series of local workshops hosted by Erin Myles and Maggie Semrau, two women on a mission to make the collective load lighter for modern women through the power of community. The workshop, entitled *Move into Kindness: unravel patterns of self-criticism to increase your emotional resilience,* was led by my dear friend Michelle Vitale, a South American, Latinx woman and an adult Third Culture Kid, born and raised in Venezuela into a Venezuelan-Italian family, and currently living in the United States.

Michelle is a psychotherapist and coach who helps people navigate change in their life and work and transform the challenges of transitions into sources of learning, possibility, and growth.

In the workshop, Michelle talked about the importance of bringing more self-compassion to ourselves when it comes to crafting new, self-affirming beliefs, with the understanding that we can't necessarily shift this overnight. She taught us that by simply adding the words, "May I..." to the beginning of an affirmation, we can ease into the truth of the statement. For example:

May I believe that I am worthy of success.

May I believe that I am worthy of happiness.

Doing this immediately takes the pressure off. We are no longer forcing ourselves to transform a deeply held belief in an instant. Instead, we can meditate on that truth and feel into it over time.

USE THESE POWER PROMPTS
What liberating truths might replace your limiting beliefs?

How might you create a self-compassionate affirmation to remind yourself about the truth of who you are?

BORROW THIS POWER STATEMENT
May I understand that I am enough and have always been enough.

2.

IGNITING YOUR TRUE POTENTIAL

4.

RESILIENCE IS A
SUPERPOWER

———

*Your experience facing and overcoming adversity
is actually one of your biggest advantages.*

—MICHELLE OBAMA

When you understand that brilliance is your birthright, you
are wildly capable, and you have always been worthy, you can
begin to explore what it looks like to fire up your potential
for the journey ahead.

After working as a marketing director in the US for five years,
I realized I was ready for a new challenge. It was the late
2000s and, thanks to the rise of social media, I had connected
with a growing community of inspirational women entrepreneurs who were leaving their corporate jobs behind them to
create a business on their own terms—without waiting for
anyone else's permission.

In 2011, I attended a workshop at a local tech conference and learned how to build my own website. In 2012, I launched a copywriting business on the side of my full-time job. And in January 2013, I had enough clients lined up and money in the bank to start working full-time for myself.

What I didn't predict was how uncertain the road ahead would be. I didn't foresee just how many highs and lows lay in wait, or that entrepreneurship would prove to be the steepest of learning curves—one that would force me to stretch myself beyond what I had thought possible.

In those first years of running my business, I had the opportunity to work with hundreds of women business owners—many of whom shared with me their vulnerable true stories of how they had turned adversity to their advantage to create a life on purpose in service of others. These women became my role models, guides, and mentors.

Time and time again, their stories showed me that the same challenging experiences and difficulties that threaten our well-being and sense of self in the present are ultimately also the same experiences and difficulties that empower us to live more meaningfully and experience greater fulfillment through personal impact.

My client, Karin Volo, is an extraordinary example of how adversity can equip and inspire us to help others. Now a writer, speaker, and trainer, she went through an ordeal many years ago that I hope none of us ever have to endure.

In 2006, everything seemed to be going beautifully for her. She had put behind her a disastrous first marriage to an abusive con man and now had a wonderful business partner and fiancé, Sergio, two delightful young daughters, as well as a successful executive recruiting business in Europe. Karin and Sergio were working hard to grow their business together and getting ready to expand into several countries. They had finally moved into their dream home and Karin was excited for the future opening up to them.

Little did she know that the darkest, toughest time of her life lay ahead.

At 6:30 a.m. on March 29, 2006, Karin was standing in line at San Diego Lindbergh International Airport with Sergio as they waited to board their homebound flight to Stockholm, Sweden. When someone tapped her on the shoulder, she turned but didn't recognize the man standing there. He looked like an ordinary traveler, but he swiftly stepped between her and Sergio as two other men in dark blue windbreakers and jeans took hold of each of her arms.

One of the men asked, "Are you Karin Volo?"

"Yes," she answered, noticing the rolled-up papers in his hand.

"I have a warrant for your arrest."

Those seven words changed the course of Karin's life.

She went on to spend the next 1,352 days—almost four years—in jail, accused of crimes involving her first husband, before her case was finally dismissed and all charges cleared.[32] By the end of this unbelievable odyssey, she had been jailed in a San Diego facility longer than any woman in its history.

What I find most remarkable about Karin's story is that, while in jail, she refused to allow herself to sink into despair. Even though fear and sadness threatened to overwhelm her on many days, she never stopped believing in the possibilities of what any of us can create for ourselves.

Instead, she worked to find ways to stay positive, arming herself with the book *Yoga for Dummies* and leading yoga classes on the roof for her fellow inmates.[33] She learned from them how to make tamales from warm water and crushed corn chips in a bag, and shared books she'd read that helped her stay in a positive state of mind.

When Karin was finally released, she says her purpose became clear, "I want to inspire others with my story and bring more joy into the world by sharing how I found courage and hope in my darkest hour."

Today, she does that through writing, speaking, and corporate training on culture, engagement, and building trust and by sharing all that she has learned on her incredible journey.

---

32   Karin Volo, "1,352 Days: An Inspirational Journey from Jail to Joy," Life with a Fabulous View, Incorporated, March 2015.

33   Georg Feuerstein and Larry Payne, *Yoga for Dummies*, For Dummies, June 2014.

From rock bottom, Karin found a way to keep her head above water and use the immense hardship she went through as fuel for finding her passion and purpose in life.

🎧 **PODCAST TIP**

Listen to my interview with Karin Volo on the *Movement Makers* podcast and learn how she found courage and hope in her darkest hour.

Visit nikkigroom.com/category/podcast/.[34]

YOUR ABILITY TO LEAD IS FORGED IN THE FIRES OF ADVERSITY.

Challenging times can ingrain in you the resilience and fortitude you need to thrive in a world of constant change and uncertainty. Not only can times like these ignite your true potential, but they can help you find courage you never knew you had and give you a profound understanding of what matters most.

Adversity helps us grow as human beings and better understand why we're on this planet in the first place. It can make us more dedicated to a specific cause or determined to do everything in our power to prevent other people from experiencing a similar level of hardship.

---

34   Nikki Groom, "An Inspirational Story from Jail to Joy," *Movement Makers* podcast, accessed on July 13, 2020.

100 STORIES WORTH TELLING

I launched the *100 Stories Worth Telling Project* in 2015 to highlight the stories of women entrepreneurs from all over the world and give them a platform from which to celebrate their experiences of thriving against the odds.[35] Each participant's story reminds us of what's possible when we refuse to give up and commit to pursuing our dreams.

One storyteller, Kate Anthony, shared how, years ago, she had been in the depths of despair and struggling to decide whether or not to leave her marriage. She said she wished she had someone—or some*thing*—that would tell her clearly, "It's time to go," or "Stay, and you'll get through this."

Sometimes her marriage had been so volatile that most people didn't want to be around her and her husband. "It was unbearable to witness," she admitted, "let alone experience."

Kate spent ten years idling in neutral at the same fork in the road, agonizing over whether they should try anything else as a couple to get them back on track. But, ultimately, she faced the truth that there was nothing else she could do and made the excruciating decision to leave.

Her painful journey made her realize how much she wanted to pay her experiences forward and help other women who found themselves in similar distressing situations. She became a certified coach and today helps women decide

---

35   Nikki Groom, "The 100 Stories Worth Telling Project," NikkiGroom. com, accessed on June 20, 2020.

whether they should stay in or leave their marriages—and then either heal their relationships or exit with grace.

"I've been to hell and back," Kate explained, "and now it's my mission in life to help other women like me get to the other side of this process with their sanity—and their hearts—intact. I'm here to help them navigate some of the toughest waters they've ever swum in and answer some of their toughest questions."

Kate turned her pain into purpose and is helping women all over the world experience more clarity, confidence, and peace of mind because of what she went through.

READ THE STORIES
Read other stories about other women who turned adversity to their advantage in the *100 Stories Worth Telling* Project, including stories from:

- **Tiffany Yu**, who survived a tragic car accident that killed her father when she was nine years old and left her with permanent damage to her right arm. Growing up without an outlet to deal with such a traumatic loss inspired Tiffany to create the community she had been missing. Today, her organization, Diversability, seeks to remove limits and barriers and empower others to build their self-confidence and self-worth.[36]

---

36   Nikki Groom, "Tiffany Yu: Rebranding Disability Through the Power of Community," *The 100 Stories Worth Telling Project*, accessed July 13, 2020.

- **Diana Malerba**, who was told that she was "too much" as a child: too passionate, too creative, and too intelligent "for a girl." After surviving a traumatic experience as a teenager, she trained as a confidence coach and NLP Master Practitioner and began to help other women advance in their careers and businesses.[37]
- **Gita Gavare Marotis**, who, at age fifteen, learned how to fire an automatic weapon, march like a soldier, and run with a gas mask on at school in Riga, Latvia. When the only world she knew collapsed, she fell into the hands of human traffickers. Years later, she decided that her experiences did not define her and began helping other women to stand up and speak their truth.[38]

Visit 100StoriesWorthTelling.com for more.

BETTER EQUIPPED TO LEAD

A life-changing diagnosis. A traumatic experience. A painful awakening.

When we are deeply affected by events in our lives, we have two choices:

We can give up, or we can get back up.

---

37   Nikki Groom, "Diana Malerba: Brave-Hearted Survivor," *The 100 Stories Worth Telling Project*, accessed July 13, 2020.

38   Nikki Groom, "Gita Gavare Marotis," *The 100 Stories Worth Telling Project*, accessed on July 13, 2020.

We can choose to see only obstacles in our way, or we can choose to see opportunities and own our power, purpose, and potential.

In the darkest of times and the hardest of moments, believing in ourselves and our ability to overcome shifts us out of hopelessness and opens the door to a whole new world of possibilities.

When author, speaker, and diversity and inclusion expert Jennifer Brown first rolled out a program called *The Gifts of LGBTQ+* for a multinational financial services company in the early days of running her consulting firm, her mission was to empower participants by helping them see that they were better equipped for leadership roles because of the identity-based challenges they'd faced and the resilience and inner strength they had developed as a result.

"The program was all about, 'I see you, I see what you've been through, and let's look at the beauty and the struggle,'" Jennifer told me. "Let's look at what you developed through the pain. Then let's think about all that you bring as a leader and as a human being to the world, and what a role model you are now. Let's put you back together in a new way so that you can go and be the light that so many others need to see."

The program was important to Jennifer because it reflected her own lived experiences. Although her close friends and family knew she was a member of the LGBTQ+ community, during her years in corporate jobs before starting her consulting company she had struggled to come out. Not seeing examples of women or LGBTQ+ professionals who she could identify with in the leadership positions she aspired to fill one day, she downplayed who she was throughout a series of professional roles. "I worried that people would like me less if they knew who I really was, or view me negatively."

The *Gifts of LGBTQ+* program years later helped Jennifer find the courage to finally show up fully. She describes the program as a critical and transformative healing process. "I know it works because it's the process that I had to go through in healing myself. That's why people get very emotional at the end."

Jennifer added that, while she has never suffered the way so many members of the LGBTQ+ community have, it's a privilege to hold space for program participants to share how resilient they've become because of their unique lived experiences of adversity and discrimination. "I don't want them to feel the shackles of that anymore."

I bet you've been through difficult circumstances too. The good news is those same circumstances have equipped you with the resilience and the fortitude and the permission you need to live your life fully, out loud, and on purpose.

Your story doesn't have to be dramatic, dangerous, or glamorous for you to find your calling in it. It can simply be the reason you get up in the morning. And you don't need to share it with anyone else, but it can be the inspiration you need to shape your goals, guide your decision-making, and do satisfying work.

USE THESE POWER PROMPTS

What have you survived in your life?

Are there any experiences that inspired you to do the work you do today?

How have the challenges you've faced better equipped you for this work?

BORROW THIS POWER STATEMENT

May I accept that I did the best I could with what I had at the time and release all self-judgment.

5.

THERE ARE NO WRONG PATHS

———

You're not defined by what somebody says is a failure for you because failure is there to point you in a different direction.

—OPRAH WINFREY

While it's true that we can find meaning in our stories and even a sense of purpose, unearthing them can surface shame that we struggle to know what to do with.

None of us are born ashamed. Shame is a learned emotion. It's the direct result of receiving a message from the outside world that we don't belong because we don't measure up somehow.

We can pinpoint shame in any feelings we have of *not enough*-ness or *too much*-ness.

For example:

I'm not good enough.
I'm too fat.
I'm not beautiful enough.
I'm too old.
I'm not likable enough.
I'm too aggressive.

And the list goes on.

A child once described shame as "a form of sadness," and I can't think of a more accurate description.[39] That sadness is rooted in a belief that we're not worthy enough to connect in a meaningful way with others. We worry that people will find out about our *not enough*-ness or *too much*-ness and reject us, and so we turn our shame inward, cover up the parts of ourselves that we don't want anyone else to see, and find reasons to hate ourselves. It's no coincidence that shame is often lurking behind mental and emotional problems like depression, anxiety, eating disorders, and substance use disorders.[40]

As women, we often feel shame for putting ourselves first, for expressing out loud what we want; for setting healthy

---

39   Simona Giordano, "Understanding the Emotion of Shame in Transgender Individuals—Some Insight from Kafka," *Life Sciences, Society and Policy*, published October 2018.

40   Vienna Miller-Prieve, "Women, Shame, and Mental Health: A Systematic Review of Approaches in Psychotherapy," retrieved from Sophia, the St. Catherine University repository website, published May 2016.

boundaries. And so our shame shows up in our silence, in our people pleasing, in our slow-burning resentment.

You can feel shame because of the way you look or don't look, the way you act or don't act, the way you speak or don't speak. You can feel shame because of the work you do or don't, the money you have or have not, the mistakes you make, the marriage you leave, the wedding you never had in the first place.

But as Elizabeth Cronise McLaughlin, the founder of The Gaia Project for Women's Leadership, once said to me, "That baggage belongs to the patriarchy, and it's time we gave it back."[41]

We experience shame when we do things outside societal norms—if we drop out of college, skip the family, or don't stay home with the kids. And we experience shame when we don't measure up to an idealized identity because of our gender, weight, age, race, ethnicity, sexual orientation, gender identity, physical or mental ability, and so on.

But when we find it in ourselves to release shame and bravely show up as the human beings we were always destined to be, we have a real opportunity to make a bigger impact.

WORTHY OF BEING SEEN AND CARED FOR

As a teen, Lindley Ashline was bullied for being different. She was a size eighteen when the "fat" taunts started in earnest. "I

---

41   Nikki Groom, "Elizabeth Cronise McLaughlin: Becoming a Powerful Force for Change," *Movement Makers* podcast, accessed on June 20, 2020.

couldn't shake the terrible, shrinking feeling in the pit of my stomach that something was wrong with me," she admitted.[42]

The trauma of that experience meant Lindley spent much of her teens and early twenties wearing the cheapest, baggiest clothing she could find, ashamed of her body and certain she needed to hide it. "I thought that someday, when one of my diets finally worked, I'd be 'good enough' to wear normal clothes and worthy of being seen. It was a miserable existence."

Then, at twenty-seven, Lindley discovered body positivity: a social movement rooted in the belief that all human beings should have a positive body image while challenging how society presents and views the physical body. It changed her entire world. "It was the first time anyone had ever told me that I might just be a worthy human being. That I didn't have to hate myself. That I didn't have to dedicate my life to changing my appearance."

Best of all, Lindley realized that she was *already* beautiful—and had always been. After spending her life hiding behind a camera lens, she realized how sad it was that she had been using her talent for photography to hide from herself. So she started deliberately seeking out the spotlight, even in small ways.

"I finally took the voice lessons I'd been too afraid to start. I began taking hundreds of selfies. I had portraits taken by a professional photographer. I pursued photography as a career after spending years believing I was 'too fat' to do that."

---

42   Nikki Groom, "Lindley Ashline: Discovering My Body Positivity," *The 100 Stories Worth Telling Project*, accessed June 20, 2020.

When she started using her camera to tell the stories of women like her, she realized the stories of so many other people needed to be told as well. Women of color. Transgender women. Agender people. More and more and more.

Today, Lindley runs a portrait and boudoir photography studio in Seattle called Sweet Amaranth. She's also changing the visual stories told in advertising and the media by creating the world's largest stock image collection focused solely on minority groups. It's called *Diverse Stock Photos* and it shares the stories of people in the LGBTQIAP+, body positive, fat acceptance, person of color (POC), and eating disorder recovery communities. "I want people to know that the body they have, right at this second, is worthy of being seen and cared for and treated like the precious vehicle for their life that it is."

So many of us walk around this world carrying deep shame about who we are and worrying about whether or not we'll be accepted—and the heartbreaking truth is we live in a world in which not everyone *is*. That's what makes Lindley's story so powerful. She not only freed herself from negative self-talk but has made it her mission to spread a message of body positivity far and wide so that others realize how beautiful they are too. Her story about defying expectations has given her a mission and a sense of purpose and connected her to a movement that is empowering others to reclaim their self-image.

So many of us are constantly being told that we're too much of this or too much of that. If we don't look like a supermodel, then we're lacking somehow. I can easily list all the ways I don't measure up physically. My nose isn't straight. My knees are too round. My hands are too big. And the list goes on. We carry this shame about not measuring up like baggage around with us—as though we are doomed to a lifetime of feeling less than. But the moment we let go of any expectations about who we should be and embrace who we are is the moment we free ourselves to create a different reality.

HOPE AND A WAY OUT

Brigitte Thériault grew up socially economically disadvantaged with an alcoholic father. "He loved me deep down and he wasn't a mean drunk," she wrote, but his addiction caused her some deep wounds.[43]

At a young age, she was searching for love, connection, and a sense of belonging. Her father was spending his days downing Molson, and their dilapidated, filthy, smoke-filled farmhouse made Brigitte feel like she constantly had dirt crawling underneath her skin. These circumstances, along with her grandmother's death when Brigitte was thirteen, destroyed Brigitte's ability to feel anything but anger and resentment.

She left high school at age fifteen after getting a job at a strip club and being put to work as a dancer. "This is something no fifteen-year-old should ever have to see or do," she admitted, "but I was wounded, and I wanted money, attention, and love."[44]

---

43   Brigitte Thériault, "How to Use Your Story to Find Your Life Purpose," *Purpose Fairy*, published October 2013.

44   Ibid.

Brigitte's quest for connection and belonging may have been futile, but that experience led her to discover that nothing made her happier than making three hundred dollars and then spending that money on a long, lavish restaurant dinner with her boyfriend. "Food became a distraction from real life. It made me feel cultured, connected, and alive."[45]

In the club, Brigitte was learning about the dark, twisted crevices of human sexuality. In restaurants, she was learning about the sensuality of food—of how a slice of hot buttered bread washed down with a glass of red wine could take her mind off everything.

Ultimately, she enrolled in cooking school and moved to New York City to follow her dream of becoming a personal chef. "Cooking school saved my life," she told me. "It gave me hope and a way out of my destructive past."[46]

It took Brigitte thirty-three years to realize she didn't have to feel ashamed about her unconventional path through life anymore. "I was doing the best I could with what I knew. You have to realize that you are not alone, it's not your fault, and we all have things to work on and move through."[47]

---

45   Brigitte Thériault, "How the Love of Food Saved My Life," *Daily Plate of Crazy*, published January 2016.

46   Thériault, *Purpose Fairy*.

47   Nikki Groom, "Brigitte Thériault: Cooking Her Way to a New Life," *The 100 Stories Worth Telling Project*, accessed June 20, 2020.

Society so often teaches us to be ashamed of who we are and what we've done in our lives—out of necessity, out of choice, and even when we've had no choice.

In her book, *The Gifts of Imperfection,* Brené Brown wrote, "Shame keeps worthiness away by convincing us that owning our stories will lead to people thinking less of us."[48]

Brigitte chose to shed this shame by beginning to share her story openly in multiple articles and interviews online and found that it helped dissolve the emotional charge around what she'd been through as a teenager.

When we *own* our stories and release any old narratives that no longer serve who we're becoming, we override the conditioning that only wants to keep us small and open the gates for more meaningful connections with people who want to see our authentic selves and accept us as we are.

TAKE ACTION

If you're ready to let go of shame stories from your past, you don't have to start by sharing them publicly, unless you feel ready to. Sometimes simply confiding to a friend or sharing with a therapist or small, intimate group can lift the burden of shame off your shoulders and help you heal.

---

48   Brené Brown, "The Gifts of Imperfection: Let Go of Who You Think You're Supposed to Be and Embrace Who You Are," Hazelden Publishing, 2010.

Sharing your story unapologetically has the power to free other people too. But before you do that, consider your answer to the following question:

When you think about the people who will receive your story, and you think about what they might be struggling with and how they might be feeling, what do you want them to know?

Answering this question will help you tell your story with purpose and wrap it around an unforgettable message that will stay with your audience long after you've shared it with them.

RADICAL SELF-ACCEPTANCE

Success is rarely a straight line. You will often take detours in your life, starting along one road and ending up on another—and that's okay. You might be tempted to treat these detours as failures, but everything that happens to us has something to teach us. Our missteps help us grow in ways we wouldn't have otherwise.

And yet what is the first thing we often do when things don't go the way we hoped? We judge ourselves. We feel ashamed and inadequate.

After Geniece Brown was hired for a corporate job in her last semester of college, she felt on top of the world. But throughout the six years that she worked there, she found herself being drawn to entrepreneurial people and ideas. "They ignited a spark in my heart," she told me.[49]

She began reading everything she could find on entrepreneurship to see what it would mean for her to start a business supporting others as a virtual assistant and online content creator. It wasn't long before she found herself writing a resignation letter. She had a handful of clients lined up already and figured she could find more once she was full time with all the extra time she'd have.

"Little did I know that the next few years would be some of the lowest points in my entire life," she admitted. "I never factored in that I would need to be prepared for all the ups and downs and clients moving on, or that I would have to market myself consistently."

Geniece's husband was working a traditional job, which helped. But Geniece's unstable income meant they couldn't live at the same financial level as when she had a guaranteed salary. "I had to get a job making about three quarters less than what I was making from my corporate job, and I felt so ashamed."

Once the dust settled and Geniece came to terms with her new normal, she became content with working two jobs at a time and gave up on her business plan for a few months. "Although I kept a positive attitude, I still felt a huge amount of shame on the inside, especially every time I ran into

---

49   Nikki Groom, "Geniece Brown: No Shame in My Game," *The 100 Stories Worth Telling Project,* accessed June 20, 2020.

someone from my old job who would ask how the business was going. I would tell them it was going great, even though it wasn't."

Eventually, Geniece returned to her original business idea and redefined her services in a way that worked for her before taking on clients once more. "I started to grow into myself and realized I could be proud about what I'd accomplished and the risks I'd taken, without shame or explanation."

Geniece had dismissed the local business market for a while, but when she realized that people in the community wanted to help and support her, she began making a point of supporting them too. Since then, she has won an award for her services, receives more referrals than ever, and her revenue has increased year on year.

"I can actually pay my monthly expenses now," she told me, "and if I ever feel like I need to work a part-time gig or event to boost my business or accelerate paying down any debt in the future, there's no shame in my game—not anymore."

Geniece's story is a great reminder that there are ups and downs and pursuing your dreams can require a lot of patience and years of hard work. It's not for the faint of heart, there is no blueprint, and there are no overnight successes.

Like Geniece, you might launch a business and find it doesn't immediately make sense to quit your day job. There's no shame in that.

When I was going through a hard time in my business, I reached out to other women business owners in a private Facebook group who I thought might understand some of the challenges that I was up against. It was liberating to hear they knew of other people who had gone back into the corporate world to raise funds to continue working toward their dreams. And it was also deeply saddening to learn how many of these women had kept their journey a secret, not wanting to deal with the shame associated with admitting they hadn't been as financially successful as quickly as they had initially hoped.

Similarly, changing careers often requires that we take a step back to go forward. You may have to go down a rung on the ladder to learn a new skill set. You may need to get a job at a different company in a different field to be happy—and that's okay too. Because the truth is, life doesn't always look the way we're taught it should. In fact, it rarely does. It can look messy. It can be at odds with someone else's image of success. And that's nothing to be ashamed of.

When I interviewed Tara McMullin, the founder and CEO of What Works, a top small business podcast and community for small business owners, for this book, she admitted she didn't use to share vulnerable things with her audience because she used to think she had to appear like she knew everything, especially because so much of her business was built around being an authority.

"I think this is part of women's conditioning because we live in a world where women are questioned faster—our credibility is questioned faster; our authority is questioned faster—and

I was trying to look as buttoned up and as polished and as professional as possible so that I wasn't questioned."

But a couple of years ago, Tara started to let go of that. She realized it was more important to show up as herself as opposed to showing up as a caricature of what an authority "should" look like. And these days, she has no problem saying, "Yes, I've got a lot of stuff figured out. I do not have all of it figured out by any stretch of the imagination, and let me tell you about some of the specific things I don't have figured out."

For example, when she changed her business model, she decided to share on social media how it was a big hit to her income. "For the first time in ten years, not only was I not paying an exorbitant sum of money to the federal government, but I got a refund."

The story was hard for her to tell—especially because, in previous years, the status of taking home a certain income or generating a certain annual revenue from her business had been a mark of her credibility, authority, identity, and sense of worthiness as an individual. To admit she didn't have that status mark anymore was a big deal for Tara. "For a long time, I worried if people found out that I wasn't making as much money anymore, they wouldn't trust me, they wouldn't listen to me, they wouldn't want to listen to the podcast, and they certainly wouldn't want to join our community."

But, in fact, the opposite was true. Tara's willingness to be transparent has helped build her community's trust in her because they feel certain she'll never lead them astray. And by recognizing how shame was robbing her self-worth and choosing to own her story, she is role modeling to her community the importance of radical self-acceptance—no matter what.

USE THESE POWER PROMPTS

Where is shame keeping you stuck and preventing you from moving forward in your life or business?

Can you identify which societal expectations this shame is rooted in?

What steps will you take to start releasing your shame stories?

BORROW THIS POWER STATEMENT

I release the shame of my past and accept all of who I am, so I can step into the promise of my future.

6.

IT'S OKAY TO NOT HAVE IT ALL FIGURED OUT

———

You don't have to know what your
purpose is to make a difference.

—ANDRÉA RANAE JOHNSON

Instead of worrying about finding a single life purpose, I encourage the women entrepreneurs in the Movement Makers Mastermind to stay open to the process of discovery.

You can do that too.

That means noticing the work that lights you up and aligns with your most important values. It means playing to your core strengths, uncovering what energizes you, and catalyzing positive change in your organization, business, or community.

Your purpose is often the sweet spot between your values, your passions, and your strengths. In other words:

- What and who matters most to you.
- What you love to do.
- What comes easily to you.

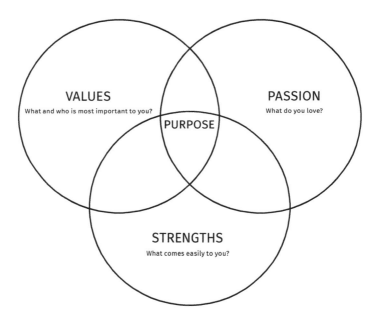

Your purpose is often the sweet spot between your values, your passions, and your strengths.

You don't have to have everything figured out to live a life on purpose. And you most certainly don't need to be a perfect human being.

In December 2013, I had been in business as a full-time free-lance copywriter for almost a year. Earlier that year, I'd found the courage to double my rates, which meant I was earning more and slowing the rate at which I was taking on new clients. But there was still a gaping void in my work. I had been helping other women leaders find the link between *their* work and purpose, but I still couldn't put my finger on *my* "Why." From the outside looking in, my business seemed like it was doing well. I was booking out for months at a time, but I was still trying to extract a deeper sense of meaning from my work.

When I won the chance to have a coaching call with award-winning author and serial entrepreneur Jonathan Fields, it felt like the best possible timing.

Jonathan theorizes that we're all born with a certain imprint for work that makes us come alive, work that lets us wake up in the morning and know, deep down, we're doing what we're here to do, "work that sets us ablaze with purpose and, fully-expressed in a healthy way, becomes a mainline to meaning, a pathway to that transcendent state of flow, and a gateway to connection and joy."[50]

We discover that imprint—our purpose—by learning first-hand what work weighs us down or, conversely, lights us up; by letting go of perfectionism and experimenting with uncertainty, however uncomfortable it might be.

---

50   Jonathan Fields, "What if You Could Discover the Work You're Here to Do, Then Spend the Rest of Your Life Doing It?" accessed June 21, 2020.

But when I got on the phone with Jonathan and he asked how he could help, I struggled to put my frustration into words. "I guess, I don't know... I just want to figure out what my *thing* is."

It sounded lame, and I kicked myself for not being more succinct, but my "thing" felt like everything to me. It felt like once I found it—my purpose, my calling, my reason for being—a pilot light would suddenly be switched on in my heart and my life would suddenly take on new meaning. I would better understand why my work mattered. I would have a mission to call my own and be inspired to persevere, no matter what.

I longed to have it all figured out: the edges of my business smoothed off, my next steps mapped out, the answers piled up in my lap and ready to roll. But Jonathan suggested I try something else instead. "What if you made next year 'The Year of Experimentation'?" he asked me, "and treated everything as if it were an experiment?"

His advice felt liberating to me, like a door had opened that I had never known existed.

FINDING TIME TO EXPERIMENT

With an open mind, I began running tests in my business all the way through 2014 to get a truer sense of where and how I could be of most service.

That year, I said yes a lot. In fact, I said yes to writing copy for fifty different business owners in fifty-two weeks. Saying yes so many times allowed me to increase my revenue, pay my bills, and increase the number of people spreading the word about my services. But slowly, it also submerged me in resentment. I was saying yes to so much that I was effectively saying no to my well-being and happiness.

In his book, *The Small Business Life Cycle*, productivity expert Charlie Gilkey calls this the third stage of being in business for yourself. "Stage three is the Crucible stage," he wrote. "You're at the delightfully frustrating point at which you're booked solid and working at full steam, but the demand for your goods and services outstrips your ability to meet it. Something has to give."[51]

You finally have to start saying no because you're already at capacity.

This applies if you're working for an organization too. When we slip into people-pleasing mode, it's easy to keep saying yes to more and more and more until our plate is full to overflowing with equally pressing "priorities." The problem with this is there's no room for creativity and little space to try something new.

Around this time, I reconnected with my smart and generous friend, Marie Poulin, the cofounder of creative digital agency Oki Doki Digital, which focuses on helping business owners level up their digital systems, workflow, and productivity so they can spend more time on what matters most. Marie shared with me that she had fallen into a similar

---

51   Charlie Gilkey, *The Small Business Lifecycle,* Jetlaunch, 2013.

trap when she was first designing and developing websites for clients. "I wasn't giving myself or my business time to breathe between projects," she explained. "I wasn't giving myself room to grow."

And so, for eight months, Marie started saying no to every new project that came in. "It was hard! There were some exciting projects I would have loved to take on, but I knew I couldn't give them my best. I told new prospective clients that if they were interested in working together, they could get back in touch with me in the spring—and to my surprise, some of them actually did!"[52]

Marie's story helped me realize that giving myself room to breathe between projects and resisting the urge to book my schedule up for months at a time would allow me to get intentional about my decision-making and the people I worked with so I could start being more proactive about building a life and business on purpose.

"For the first time in five years of running a business, I now consistently have evenings and weekends free to do what I want to do," Marie said. "I don't wake up feeling panicked anymore about what I need to accomplish."

I didn't start turning projects down immediately. I didn't want to miss out on any opportunities. But as soon as I began doing so, I felt more in control of my business than I ever had. I discovered that saying no is addictive in the most

---

52   Marie Poulin, "Are You Booking Your Clients Too Far in Advance?" MariePoulin.com, accessed June 20, 2020.

empowering of ways. And I finally had the space I needed to envision what was next for me. I felt sure if I followed my heart and my gut, and if I continued to experiment and try different ways of being of service to people while playing to my strengths, my purpose would unfold over time.

The following year, while I was quiet on the front end of my business, I was busy behind the scenes. I tested new offerings that never even made it onto my website. I increased my prices and didn't announce it to the world. I flirted with the idea of creating a new service and, later, a new program. In the end, inundated with client work, the program wound up in the "someday" pile, but I decided that was okay... because progress is not perfection.

As it turned out, all these tiny experiments helped me clarify what I wanted to do (and what I didn't want to do) next. I discovered that giving myself the permission I needed to play was the radical shift I so desperately needed. It took the pressure off completely. And it helped me tap into ideas I might never have explored otherwise.

This process taught me that failure isn't fatal. Far from it, in fact. Instead, it's an opportunity to adapt, pivot, and emerge with clarity, resolve, and a renewed focus for the future.

Not knowing what our purpose is today doesn't negate the work we do tomorrow. We can still be of service. We can still use our gifts and our strengths and our values to inform how we help others. And we can practice getting comfortable with the distinctly uncomfortable idea that our purpose may not reveal itself to us all at once, but piece by tiny piece:

a conversation we have here, a book we read there, a podcast we listen to over there—a series of tiny epiphanies that nudge open the door to a future where we get to exercise our full potential.

While slower growth can make us feel impatient or like we're on the wrong track, finding your purpose isn't something that needs to be rushed—and changes in direction are often necessary so we can learn what we want and don't want more of in our lives.

The beauty is in the unfolding.

And in the meantime, we can choose to open our minds to the possibilities in front of us, resolve to follow the clues, and learn to find joy in the journey.

GETTING COMFORTABLE WITH UNCERTAINTY

I often share Jonathan's advice with my clients because I think it's an important reminder that the path to purpose isn't necessarily linear. And an almost-immediate way to take the pressure off our shoulders is to remind ourselves that we *don't* have to have all the answers figured out from day one. Not only that, but our purpose can evolve over time, as we uncover more of what matters most to us.

Often when we say we're searching for clarity, in reality we're searching for certainty. Certainty makes us feel like we can accomplish the impossible, while uncertainty makes us feel afraid and insecure. In his book, *Uncertainty: Turning Fear and Doubt into Fuel for Brilliance,* Jonathan Fields writes about how uncertainty can keep us from taking the risks necessary to do great work and craft a deeply-rewarding life.[53] But the longer we're willing to live in the questions that uncertainty surfaces, the more likely we are to come up with better and more creative answers.

During a workshop led by brand and culture advisor Steven Morris at a retreat, I learned that these types of questions are called "beautiful questions," and they can help guide us in times of uncertainty.[54]

Beautiful questions have the power to reorient our life's trajectory. They open us up to moments of truth and the practice of pivoting or evolving. What differentiates these questions is that they can't be answered immediately. Rather, we must be willing to live with them for a while until the answer presents itself to us.

These beautiful questions help us see that wading through the unknown is a gift and an opportunity, a time to be patiently curious as we learn to trust that the answers will reveal themselves at just the right moment.

BEAUTIFUL QUESTIONS SHOULD:
- Be ambitious and actionable.
- Cause you to reassess your assumptions.

---

53   Jonathan Fields, *Uncertainty: Turning Fear and Doubt into Fuel for Brilliance*, Portfolio; Reprint edition, 2012.

54   Jenny Blake, "Beautiful Questions for Challenging Times with Steve Morris," *Pivot Podcast,* released March 29, 2020.

- Be impossible to answer immediately.
- Spark breakthrough ideas.
- Create a more fulfilled *you*.

Treating life like an experiment helps us make faster decisions by getting us out of analysis paralysis and into action. Each instance of uncertainty reminds us to tap into our inner power and rise to the occasion.

By conducting a series of tiny experiments, we get to focus on progress, not perfection, as we design the life we want. Even when our experiments "fail," we can use those setbacks as data to guide our future successes. We can fail forward.

As Zen Habits blogger Leo Babauta writes, "We get paralyzed because we're fretting about making the perfect choice—and worried about making the wrong choice. It's a little micro-moment of perfectionism."[55]

The key, says Leo, is not seeing our decisions as final. "With an experiment, you run a test and see what the results are. If you don't get good results, you can try another option and run another test. Then you can see what the outcomes of the choices are (the info you didn't have when first thinking about the decision), and you can make a better-informed decision now."

In this way, working becomes research.

---

55   Leo Babauta, "Easier Decision-Making: Conduct Experiments," Zen Habits (blog), accessed June 21, 2020.

A bigger-picture perspective also helps here, Leo explained. "Experiments might take months, or a year—that's a tiny amount of time in the space of a lifetime, and those bigger experiments are worth learning about."

When we remove the pressure to figure everything out today, we can move into immediate action with curiosity, integrity, and intention. We can lead in a way that reflects what and who is most important to us.

When you expand your thinking, reconcile yourself with the past, and break through any limiting beliefs that have been holding you back, you can begin to activate your full potential and become more intentional about the impact you want your life to have.

USE THESE POWER PROMPTS
What's at the sweet spot between your values, passions, and strengths? Can you find any clues about the type of work that would feel purposeful, fulfilling, and impactful to you?

What would happen if you began to treat your work as an experiment? Which tests would you run and why?

BORROW THIS POWER STATEMENT
May I grant myself the space to experiment and know that it's okay not to have all the answers.

3.

GETTING INTO ACTION

7.

YOU DON'T HAVE TO BE PERFECT

———

Failing isn't the end. It's just part of the process.

—STACI JORDAN SHELTON

It was early 2016 and I'd just released the first few episodes of my podcast, *Movement Makers*. I launched it because I wanted to showcase in-depth conversations and unfiltered stories from successful business leaders making a difference on the planet. I'd been tapping my network for guests to come onto the show—many of whom I considered mentors—and, to my surprise, almost everyone I had asked said yes.

My friend Deb had left me a voice note after listening to one of my interviews. She wanted to let me know how much she'd enjoyed our discussion. "I listened to the whole interview in the car with a friend. I'm in complete awe of what you're doing. You are killing it!" she said.

I relished the praise. I was proud of the podcast and excited to be sharing my favorite people with listeners. I felt like the interviews could almost be considered a free crash course in business from some of the brightest minds in entrepreneurship. I had hired a podcast producer, had some fancy cover art designed, and recorded a nifty little jingle to kick off each episode.

Deb's voice note stroked my ego. It made me feel good about myself and what I'd accomplished. It felt like validation and like I was finally on the right path.

Later that day, I was driving back home after running an errand. I desperately needed a gas station, but foolishly thought I had enough juice to make it over the bridge. *Uh oh, not so fast.* My car stuttered to a halt on the upward curve of the bridge, and traffic immediately began to stack up behind me—unable to pass because of the oncoming traffic. Helplessly, I called AAA, and, soon enough, police arrived and began directing vehicles around me while I cowered in shame.

I was totally embarrassed and frustrated at myself for causing a scene—not to mention humiliated about not having any cash on me to pay the AAA guy back for the gas when he arrived. But when I finally reached home, my humiliation had hardened into what I can only describe as resolve. I decided I wanted to share my story on social media as a reminder that, on the same day, things can be both good and bad and easy and hard. And that's normal and human and nothing to be ashamed of—it's all just part of the journey.

And then some days, right after someone tells you you're killing it, you run out of gas on the Mount Hope Bridge. This is real life, folks, I posted.

Ack! That's always been a nightmare of mine. Hope it all got resolved quickly, one friend replied.

I had a bad day too. Tomorrow will be better, another reassured me.

That happened to me on that bridge when I was a teenager, confessed another.

Just life making you stop and enjoy the moment, suggested someone else.

When you're killing it, the little things like gas aren't important. Your brain has better things to do. Today is a new day and you have a full tank!

At the very least, I amused some folks that afternoon. But by telling the truth about the day's events, I hoped I could somehow normalize the idea that it's okay for us to screw up. I shared my experience later that week when I interviewed K. C. Carter, a mindfulness teacher, for the podcast.

"If we're going to be people of authenticity, we have to be respectful of the power that we wield," he responded, "and that means being an example, being willing to embarrass ourselves publicly, showing our flaws because it gives people permission to do the same. People *need* that permission to fail."[56]

It made me realize how much of the time the cultural narratives we're exposed to dance around the truth. They dance around our imperfect lives and make us believe we're somehow falling short—and that is simply not the case.

When you give yourself permission to fail, you break the hold that any limiting beliefs from your past may have had over your future. You get to be you, unapologetically. And when you no longer allow perfectionism to call the shots, *everything* changes. You become a shining example of what it means to be fulfilled and free.

If you're feeling depleted from constantly battling with external influences that keep you from embracing your most authentic self, I want you to know that you're not alone. We are *all* battling these tides, every single day. And it's okay if you fall short. And it's okay if your journey doesn't look the way other people think it's supposed to. And it's okay if you make mistakes. You're only human, after all.

🎧 **PODCAST TIP**

Listen to my interview with K. C. Carter on the *Movement Makers* podcast when we talk about why it's important that we share the vulnerable true stories of our human experiences and give other people permission to fail.

---

56   Nikki Groom, "KC Carter: Give Yourself Permission to Glow in the Dark," *Movement Makers* podcast, accessed July 13, 2020.

Visit nikkigroom.com/category/podcast/.[57]

IT'S OKAY TO FAIL

The daughter of immigrants, Reshma Saujani spent her entire life thinking that the more perfect version of herself would be the smarter version of herself and the happier version of herself.[58] But at thirty-three, she woke up with a jolt and realized how miserable she had become. Every day, she came home from her job as a hedge-fund lawyer and ended up in the fetal position with a large glass of wine.

"I felt like I was stuck," she admitted. "I ended up running for Congress because it was something that I had dreamed about doing since I was thirteen years old but had been too afraid to do because I was worried that I would fail."[59]

Not only was Reshma the first Indian American woman to run for Congress, but she also ran against an incumbent in New York City in the primary, which, she confesses, was a total no-no in 2010. She did it anyway.

"Before that, I was so focused on doing everything perfectly. This was the first time that I really put myself out there and took a risk, knowing it might not work out. It was the most amazing ten months of my life because I finally felt free."[60]

---

57   Ibid.

58   Leah Carroll, "The Founder of Girls Who Code Wants Women to Lose (and Win)," *Refinery 29*, published March 6, 2019.

59   Ibid.

60   Carroll, *Refinery 29*.

Reshma lost the New York primary but discovered the most interesting thing about losing was that it didn't break her. She remembered thinking, *I'm not broken. I failed and I'm not broken. I didn't die.*

Not only did Reshma learn that failure didn't kill her, but she discovered it made her stronger and braver. When she had recovered from the initial disappointment of losing the New York primary, she realized no part of her wanted to go back to the private sector. Instead, she wanted to serve people in a bigger way.

Over time, she came up with the idea to launch Girls Who Code, a nonprofit organization created to support and increase the number of women in computer science by equipping young women with computing skills. Despite not knowing how to code herself, Reshma found the courage to start anyway, and by 2019, Girls Who Code had reached over 185,000 girls across all fifty states in the US, Canada, and the United Kingdom—with 50 percent of those girls coming from historically underrepresented groups.

"Far too often, we think that we have to be experts in the thing when we begin," said Reshma.[61] But her story shows that you don't have to have it all figured out to follow your heart and just start.

Reshma said the idea for her book, *Brave Not Perfect: Fear Less, Fail More, and Live Bolder,* came from a TED Talk she gave a few years prior. "I made the point that we teach our

---

61   Ibid.

girls to be perfect and we teach our boys to be brave, and that this perfectionism training has real consequences in our adult lives. And that message really struck a nerve."[62]

YOU MIGHT DISCOVER YOU'RE A PERFECTIONIST IF:

- You try to do too much by setting unattainable goals—only to feel major self-doubt after not accomplishing what you set out to do.
- You worry that you're not "cut out for" the work you want to do and constantly compare yourself to other people who you think better fit the mold for success.
- You struggle to delegate work to anyone else for fear that they won't measure up to your exacting standards.
- Success doesn't feel all that satisfying because you're always looking ahead to the next milestone and the next.
- You feel like you're failing yourself and others by always falling short.

If you recognize yourself in any one of these statements, I'm right there with you. I have absolutely experienced what it means to overstretch, compare myself, and give myself a hard time for not doing more, more, more.

But we have to realize that failing doesn't say anything about our capacity to try again. In fact, every time we fail, it teaches us something new—about ourselves, about our work, about why we're here, about what we need to learn or how we need to grow.

62   Carroll, *Refinery 29*.

We become perfectionists because we believe our value is contingent on what we achieve or don't achieve. But we are valuable regardless of what we do or don't do.

My worth isn't tied to being perfect, and neither is yours.

When we reach for a goal that at once scares and excites us, there is no guarantee that things will work out exactly the way we hope. Our sometimes unrealistic expectations set us up for self-blame because we can never experience the perfect results we set out to. As a result, we grow wary, less productive, less brave. We may even stop trying to succeed altogether or sabotage our success because we're too afraid that things won't go the way we hope.

No wonder perfectionism has been repeatedly linked to stress, overwhelm, reduced creativity, burnout, anxiety, depression, and other problems. Our self-defeating tendencies are sucking the joy out of our lives—and it doesn't help that they make us less likely to ask for help and so limit our access to the kind of support we need most when we're giving ourselves a hard time.

The good news is you can unlearn perfectionism by learning how to be braver now.

Here are a few ideas to get you started:

1. **Be realistic.**

Stop with the all-or-nothing approach and instead work on setting S.M.A.R.T. goals (Specific, Measurable, Attainable,

Relevant, and Time-Bound) that have realistic outcomes. Reduce anxiety by breaking any overwhelming and high-stakes projects into smaller steps that allow you to focus on one task at a time.

2. See failure for what it is.

Remember, failing doesn't personally make you a failure. Learn to take your mistakes in stride and start seeing failure as the learning opportunity it is. Push yourself to act before you're ready and ask yourself, *What data can I mine from my experiences, even when things don't go according to plan? What lessons did I learn and how might they inform my next steps?* Failing forward in this way can be a liberating way to live and help you find the path you're meant to follow through life.

3. Step outside your comfort zone regularly.

Sticking to what's safe and familiar will never get you where you want to go. Instead, practice being imperfect—whether that means not giving yourself a hard time for the typo in that email you just sent to a client, not beating yourself up for a product launch that didn't go according to plan, or admitting you don't have all the answers. Remember, "good enough" really is good enough.

4. Question why you're putting so much pressure on yourself.

You can still be a high achiever while taking a more balanced approach to life. Consider cutting back on self-imposed stress by replacing pressure with gratitude. Recall all the things you've done right rather than all the things you've done wrong. Your mistakes don't ultimately matter, so release them and be careful not to use them as weapons against yourself.

5. **Remember that done is better than perfect.**

Procrastination is a symptom of perfectionism. If you notice that you're endlessly tweaking projects and never finishing them, remember that you're doing the best you can with what you have and cut yourself some slack. Practice believing in your ideas and remember that the only way to improve is by following through. Accountability can often help in this instance. You might want to find an accountability buddy, hire a coach, or join a mastermind group.

THE TROUBLE WITH SOCIAL MEDIA

I think we can all recall times in our lives when we've allowed our critical inner voice to take charge. For some reason, it's easier to compare ourselves to other people and measure our worth based on what they do—especially in a world where we can compare our messy real lives with other people's impeccably curated social media feeds at the tap of multiple apps on our phones.

We struggle with perfectionism because we compare our behind the scenes to everyone else's highlights reel.

I only need to open up Instagram to receive the message that every other small business owner in the world is doing more than me, faster than me, and better than me. And yet

I can pass whole swaths of time scrolling and scrolling and scrolling as my self-worth slowly spirals.

I know I am not alone in this.

In a blog post, *Company of One* author Paul Jarvis wrote, "I only tweet when I have something interesting, funny, or of value to share. In reality, 99 percent of my day is filled with non-interesting, non-funny stuff. I know this about myself, yet when I go online and read or see other people's stuff, I assume they're different, and somehow, their lives are awesome and interesting all of the time."[63]

When we only look at ourselves and others through rose-tinted glasses, it's no wonder we worry that our private, *real* selves fall short.

But I've learned you don't have to be perfect to be remarkable. That's why it's so refreshing when people share stories that reinforce that message.

Take Ashley Beaudin, for example. An inspirational speaker and self-sabotage coach, she founded The Imperfect Boss Movement with a mission to make imperfect normal and inspire women to be real and confident in life and at work.

Ashley remembers as clear as day the moment she decided to do something about the perfectionism that holds so many people back. "I was laying on my bed scrolling through

---

63   Paul Jarvis, "No One on the Internet Is Living the Life You Think They Are," accessed on June 22, 2020.

Instagram, and I was bombarded with these perfect images—amazing offices, best friends, six-figure-launches, and flawless fashion—and I thought to myself, *My life doesn't look anything like this. I have great moments, but I also have heartache, hard days, failure, and disappointment.* I knew I had to open up a real conversation about what it looks like to make your dreams happen so we'd realize we're not alone and be empowered to keep going."

Within three weeks, Ashley had launched a viral marketing campaign that saw the #imperfectboss hashtag sweep across social media. Her mission was to let women know they are worthy of belonging and being known up close, regardless of being imperfect.

As part of the hashtag campaign, I taped a sheet of paper to my window and took a photo that I shared to Instagram with the following words written on it in thick, black marker:

True story: I feel not good enough more often than I feel good enough.

I'm working on it.

In the caption, I admitted that I didn't realize perfection should never have been my goal in the first place, because all any of us can do is start where we are with what we have and do the best we can.

There is power in collectively sharing what's true for us. Thanks to Ashley and The Imperfect Boss Movement, bosses everywhere are publicly sharing the truth about their struggles in the messy middle of running a business more publicly. By sharing vulnerable true stories that shine a light on what it really means to be a small business owner, they are not only defying cultural expectations of perfection but liberating others from the need to pretend that they have it all together.

One by one, they are sending a clear message: *Hey, it's not just you; you're not the only one struggling with this. This is a universal struggle. I get it. Because I've been there too. And there is hope. This won't last forever.*

HIGH INTENTION, LOW ATTACHMENT

Being brave is not about being fearless. Being brave means stepping out in faith *regardless* of our fear.

Many times I have hesitated to step into action and be more visible and use my voice because I could fail in full view of everyone. But we can cultivate a different kind of relationship with fear: one rooted in compassion.

That means not suppressing our fear but, instead, *listening* to it and asking what it wants to show us. You may discover that you have knowledge gaps you need to fill to move forward, or underlying anxieties that attach to past experiences and once kept you safe, which you no longer need to thrive. When you have a fuller understanding of the message fear is trying to convey, you can give that fear the reassurance it needs, and take intentional action with an objective mind.

My friend Greg Faxon, a business coach and catalyst for high-performing entrepreneurs, calls this a "high intention, low attachment" mindset.[64] In other words:

- You set goals and take action with the highest of intentions, but you don't over-invest emotionally in the outcome or allow it to affect your self-esteem, happiness, or peace of mind.
- You have a clear vision of what you want and make purposeful decisions without being distracted by limiting stories.
- You put in the right amount of effort for the right (S.M.A.R.T.) goal and have faith that everything will work out the way it's supposed to.

At the same time, you mindfully detach from the chain of events that your actions set in motion and don't take the results personally. Instead, you surrender control, simply taking the right next step and the right next step and trusting that all the pieces will fall into place when and where and how they're supposed to.

While high intention, low attachment is the goal, when intentionality is lacking we can grow apathetic, or when we're too attached to the outcome we can become needy and feel like a victim when things don't go according to plan.

---

64   Greg Faxon, "How to Pursue Your Goals (The Right Way)," GregFaxon. com, accessed July 13, 2020.

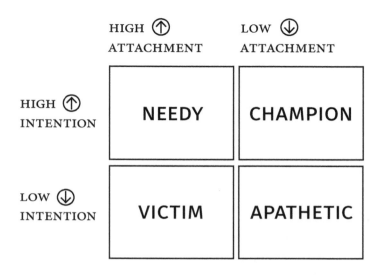

A high-intention, low-attachment mindset.[65]

When you can stop limiting your potential by giving yourself opportunities to go after what you *really* want with optimism and self-compassion, a whole new world of possibilities opens up.

You grow less and less concerned with what other people think. You no longer hold yourself back because you're afraid of failing. And you stop waiting for anyone else's permission to follow your dreams.

65   Ibid.

 **PODCAST TIP**

Listen to my interview with Greg Faxon on the *Movement Makers* podcast when we talk about high intention, low attachment, and how we can cultivate a different kind of relationship with fear—and be sure to stick around for the guided meditation at the end![66]

Visit nikkigroom.com/category/podcast/.

USE THESE POWER PROMPTS

Where has perfectionism been holding you back?

What do you think your fear might be trying to tell you? How can you work with that fear to make progress toward your goals?

Where could you practice high intention, low attachment in your life or business?

BORROW THIS POWER STATEMENT

May I remember that my worth is not tied to being perfect.

---

66   Nikki Groom, "Greg Faxon: Don't Let The Fear Win," *Movement Makers* podcast, accessed July 13, 2020.

8.

SELF-CARE IS NOT SELFISH

———

Caring for myself is not self-indulgence, it is self-preservation.

—AUDRE LORDE

Kim Sutton had charged close to fifty thousand dollars to multiple credit cards to grow her freelance marketing business. Under pressure to compete with the low hourly rates of freelancers located overseas, she was undercharging for her services, and a good day meant she barely broke even. She always felt obligated to say yes to every freelance opportunity that came her way, and her chase for income had led her down a path of despair. Stuck in a scarcity mindset, she never fully believed she'd ever have enough clients, work, or money to support her husband and three kids.

Things got so bad that Kim rarely slept more than four hours a night unless she crashed from sheer exhaustion. "I was exhausted," she told me. "Not only was my family struggling financially, but I was trying to do everything in my business myself."

Not surprisingly, she began suffering from frequent anxiety attacks from the stress of owing so much money and the pressure of being the primary breadwinner for her family. When she caught herself fantasizing about driving her car off the road, she caught her train of thoughts and realized she was at a breaking point. She confessed to her husband how she had been feeling and was admitted to a psychiatric hospital for the next six days, where she racked up a multiple five-figure bill. "It was an amount that could have easily paid for multiple tropical vacations," she pointed out, "including hotels and airfare."

That experience set Kim on a new trajectory. With a renewed sense of purpose, she began saying no to clients she sensed weren't a good fit, building products and programs so she no longer had to devote 100 percent of her time to client work, and replacing her regular To Do list with a "Purposeful Prioritized Actions" list, which helped her grow her income to five figures and more a month.

Today, Kim works as a self-care, systems, and support strategist for other stressed-out women entrepreneurs. Working differently enabled her to not only earn more over time but also add ten amazing individuals to her team who not only support the business but each other. And she sleeps a full eight hours a night, every night—peacefully and without stress.

"My self-care takes precedence over all else in my life, period," she said. "I sleep knowing I am doing the best I can do. If you're struggling, please know you're not alone. All you need to do is ask for help. Neglecting self-care is not worth the price paid in the long run. I was fortunate that it only cost me tens of thousands of dollars. In the end, it could have cost me my life. Don't let your lack of self-care cost you yours."

The hustle-at-all-costs mentality—or grind culture—that Kim fell prey to is advanced by people like entrepreneur Gary Vaynerchuk, who has recommended spending eighteen hours a day working on your startup in your first year in business, and Grant Cardone, a real estate mogul who advocates working ninety-five hours a week if you want to have a chance at earning seven figures.[67]

But this culture upholds scarcity culture, which feeds on feelings of inadequacy and thrives on fear. It tells us that there is only so much available to us and that our needs don't matter, and that's simply not the case.

When we're stressed and overloaded, taking care of ourselves tends to be the first thing to go. We talk about our businesses, our personal lives, our relationships, or our families, but we never center ourselves in the conversation and ask, *What do I need? What's my capacity for things? What is my value system? What do I believe?*

---

67   Inc. Staff, "Why Startup Founders Need to Set Aside 18 Hours a Day for the First Year," *Inc.*, published November 25, 2015; Kathleen Elkins, "Self-Made Millionaires Agree on How Many Hours You Should Be Working to Succeed," Make It—CNBC.com, published June 2017.

Overwhelmed, drained, and disconnected from what we want and what we need, we burn out and become ineffective, unproductive, and disengaged. Instead, we have to learn to put our oxygen mask on first and be unapologetic about doing that.

TAKE ACTION

Take Kim's lead and convert your To Do list into a Purposeful Prioritized Actions list. Here are a few pointers to get you started:

- You can feel the impact of Purposeful Prioritized Actions years from now.
- You have no more than five projects on your Purposeful Prioritized Actions list, and they are all important to you.
- Purposeful Prioritized Actions can only be done by you; they can't be delegated to anybody else.

THE RESENTMENT REMINDER

I've learned that whenever we feel resentment seeping in, it's a sign. It signifies that we are feeling powerless, have stopped communicating what we need because we're convinced it won't matter or make a difference, and are sacrificing what's most important to us for something more important to someone *else*—someone who cares less about us as individuals and more about what we can do for them.

We feel resentful when we don't feel heard. We feel resentful when we say yes when we want to say no because we feel we don't have a choice. We feel resentful when we give too much for too little. We feel resentful when we stretch ourselves beyond our immediate capacity. We feel resentful in the face of injustice.

Resentment shows us our boundaries and reflects our worth. It's a reminder and a message that something has to change. When I was working seven days a week because I needed the money, I could feel the resentment bubbling up and roiling around in my chest.

I've since learned that burnout looks a lot like resentment. Work begins to feel increasingly stressful and frustrating. We grow cynical about the way we're being asked to work or the people we're working with. Sometimes we numb out because we're distancing ourselves emotionally, unable to cope, and battling with feeling constantly exhausted.[68]

As an entrepreneur, I've found it's easy to get burned out because you feel like saying no is bad for business. Not only are you thinking about the income you'll generate but the opportunities that might later come along because you said yes. I once offered to work for free for one of my dream clients for exactly this reason. I didn't have the bandwidth, but I offered anyway and ended up stressed and overwhelmed with work. In the same way, you might avoid saying no in your career in case it blocks you from a future promotion.

What makes this worse is that when you tell people how busy you are, they almost inevitably say, "Well, busy's a good thing."

68   Brigid Schulte, "Brigid Schulte: Why Time Is a Feminist Issue," *The Sydney Morning Herald*, updated March 2015.

I don't think busy *is* a good thing. But it's part of our culture to be busy, to hustle, to sacrifice ourselves for the work we do. But if we sacrifice our well-being, what good are we to anyone?

You can't have a positive impact if you're resentful, burned out, anxious, overwhelmed, stressed, or depressed.

It's simply not possible.

TIME IS A FEMINIST ISSUE

If you've ever worked in an office for someone else, you may be familiar with toxic cultures of success where the expectation is you show up early and leave late and work yourself to the bone in between. When you start your own business, it's hard to shake this conditioning and easy to treat yourself like your own worst boss—especially if you refuse to give yourself any time off, constantly overload yourself with an impossible number of tasks, and rarely pause to celebrate your accomplishments.

If you have kids at home, you may feel even more fraught because of everything you have to do.

Author Brigid Schulte had a demanding job, workaholic peers, and a whole lot of guilt that—as a working mother—she wasn't with her kids every minute of the day.[69] One of her bosses liked to say that the best workers were always in the office until nine and ten at night. Meanwhile, she had to keep

---

69   Kimberlee D'Ardenne, "Invisible Labor Can Negatively Impact Well-Being in Mothers," Arizona State University website, January 2019.

reminding herself that she loved her husband despite burning with low-level resentment whenever she did the laundry, grocery shopping, cooking, child-care drop offs, dry cleaning, bills, pediatrician appointments, and summer camp planning.

When a time-use expert told her she had thirty hours of leisure time every week, she stopped breathing. "I sat in my chair, phone to my ear, jaw open, and utterly frozen in disbelief."

When she had recovered her senses enough to speak, she sputtered, "I don't know what you're talking about. I don't have thirty hours of leisure a week."

"Yes you do," the time-use expert insisted. "Come do a time study with me, and I'll show you where your leisure is."

After the time expert looked through the messy time diaries she'd been keeping, he found twenty-seven hours of what he called *leisure*, and Brigid called *bits and scraps of garbage-y time*. "Five minutes here. Ten minutes there. Listening to the radio, exhausted, trying to get out of bed. Getting some exercise. Waiting by the side of the road for a tow truck."

She didn't realize at the time that this is what time is like for most women: fragmented and interrupted by childcare and housework. "Whatever leisure time they have is often devoted to what others want to do—particularly the kids—and making sure everyone else is happy doing it."

She came to learn that women have never had a history or culture of leisure—in contrast to men, who have enjoyed long, uninterrupted hours of leisure since the dawn of humanity—and that many women don't feel like they deserve leisure time because it would make them selfish. "Instead, they felt they had to earn time to themselves by getting to the end of a very long to-do list. Which, let's face it, never ends."

Brigid began to realize that time is power, and time is a feminist issue.

While things may be more equal now in terms of women gaining or creating meaningful employment, many have still not relinquished the traditional role of keeping house and raising their children, which means they are effectively doing the work of two people.

One study of almost 400 American married or partnered mothers found that 90 percent of the survey participants admitted to bearing sole responsibility for organizing their family's schedules.[70]Another study revealed that, on an average day, women in heterosexual relationships spent almost an hour more doing household activities than their husbands.[71] And this doesn't even take into consideration those women raising families and running businesses on their own.

My friend, burnout expert Audrey Holst, explained it this way: "The demand has doubled, and the expectation has stayed exactly the same. We don't recognize any of the invisible labor."

---

70   Ibid.

71   US Bureau of Labor Statistics, "American Time Use Survey," last modified December 2016.

A while back, performance consultant and professional encourager Staci Jordan Shelton wrote, "I hate it when people tell you, 'You have the same amount of hours in the day that Beyoncé has.' You do... but maybe not the same resources or support. Where resources and support are lacking, things don't get done quickly. It often extends the amount of time needed to make things happen. I'm thinking, *Stop asking for more time; start calling forth more support.*"

Women need to uplift and support one another, not contribute to the myth that it's possible to have and do it all. Instead of airbrushing reality, let's get real about what's on our plate.

TAKE ACTION
- In the first study mentioned above, the author urges women to have ongoing conversations with their partners about more equitably sharing the load of invisible labor and meaningfully connecting with other supportive mothers. Based on her work and research, she believes such solidarity and support helps build critical resilience in women.[72]
- You might also consider how to better surround yourself with a support system of people who can help you get things done—without leaving you feeling depleted. That's key if you want to avoid burnout, replenish your inner resolve, and remain productive. We'll dive deeper into this topic in the next chapter.

---

72   D'Ardenne, January 2019.

DOING LESS, BUT BETTER

Women's experiences and expectations around work are often compounded by the fact that we generally struggle with determining how to do the most important thing when, from the top down, everything seems important—and there is a limited number of people and time and money and resources to get everything done.

Multitasking without clear and focused priorities not only reduces productivity, but it also contributes to stress and leads to burnout. In the book *Essentialism: The Disciplined Pursuit of Less*, Greg McKeown writes, "Remember that if you don't prioritize your life, someone else will."[73]

That quote has completely transformed how I see my time and how I prioritize and block out the time I have so I can focus on meaningful work that makes me feel fulfilled, in my element, and on purpose.

One way I prioritize what's on my to-do list is to use Eisenhower's Urgent/Important principle to rank things according to whether they are:

1. Urgent and important
2. Not urgent and important
3. Not important but urgent
4. Not urgent and not important

---

73   Greg McKeown, "Essentialism: The Disciplined Pursuit of Less," Currency, April 2014.

The first group (**urgent and important**) typically takes up most of our time and energy.

The second group (**not urgent and important**) is typically comprised of our most important projects; the work most worthy of our attention that will move us forward, toward our goals.

The third group (**not important but urgent**) is typically made up of tasks that prevent us from achieving our goals and should ideally be rescheduled or delegated.

The fourth group (**not urgent and not important**) often constitutes those tasks other people have added to our plate that don't contribute to our lives or align with our objectives. These tasks can usually be set aside—often permanently.

Unless something in group one is extremely pressing and can't be put to one side, I like to start my days with my most important projects from group number two and figuring out how I want to move those forward. This work tends to feel most meaningful to me because I know it's not busy-work, but instead it's the work that will ultimately move my business forward.

PRACTICE OVER PERFECTION

Many times when I'm coaching small business owners, I'll talk about the importance of practicing healthy habits—as well as being compassionate toward ourselves if we don't make it to yoga class, or we don't wake up at the time we said we would, or we don't eat the healthiest dinner possible.

While it's true that our self-esteem rises and falls in direct proportion to the commitments we make to ourselves, we shouldn't make self-care another "must do" or beat ourselves up if we don't do it.

Instead, I'm a big believer in practice over perfection, which is the notion that you simply have to practice anchoring yourself in new ways of being, one day at a time, and prioritizing yourself and your well-being as you repeatedly stretch outside of your comfort zone.

USE THESE POWER PROMPTS

What commitments can you make to yourself when it comes to preserving your well-being?

Are there any new habits you need to cultivate? Any ways you can free up more leisure time on a regular basis?

What do you need to make that happen?

BORROW THIS POWER STATEMENT

May I not feel guilty for taking care of myself so I can do my best work.

9.

YOU DON'T HAVE
TO DO IT ALONE

———

*Realize that you are not alone, that we are in this
together, and most importantly that there is hope.*

—DEEPIKA PADUKONE

When I first started my business, I had this overwhelming
desire to find other, like-minded souls. People who could
understand some of the challenges I was up against as a new-
bie small business owner, who would have comparable experiences and different ways of seeing the road ahead. People
who could say, *This is normal because I've been there too. We
can figure this out together.*

I made it my mission early on to connect with as many small
business owners as possible, expanding my network both
online and offline, having heartfelt conversations, and always
being sure to ask at the end of our time together, "How can
I support you?"

In Rhode Island where I live, I was convinced I was in the minority. I couldn't imagine there were many other women like me, running online businesses in the smallest state in the US. So I set out to prove myself wrong. Every time I stumbled across a potential new local connection online, I would reach out and introduce myself: "Hey, I love what you're up to! I'd love to learn more about what you do!" I'd then suggest meeting up for coffee, lunch, or a glass of wine after work. Online, I would schedule a virtual call and we'd learn more about one another and promise to keep each other informed about what we were up to.

I entered each of these in-person and virtual meetups with the highest of intentions. If we connected and that individual later became a client, then great. If we connected and that individual later connected me to someone *else* who would become a client—or if I could do the same for them—then wonderful. But the true value of those meet-ups was the solidarity we built in the space of one or two hours—the kind of solidarity that only comes from people who are in the trenches *with* you, and whose ultimate success is somehow bound up with your own.

I felt like I had finally found "my people." In these connections, I found my struggles reflected. I felt less alone—and that gave me hope, courage, and the strength to continue.

When you're pursuing your dreams and doing work that matters, the ability to network strategically is a game changer. Not only can it give you new ideas, but networking with the right people can help you gain clarity and stop second-guessing yourself, not to mention business referrals and new friends.

Pushing myself out of my comfort zone over and over again to grow my circle and stay connected to that circle has almost always been worth the initial discomfort of reaching out. I'm an introvert, which means that alone time recharges my batteries and I prefer deep one-on-one conversations versus superficial chats at networking events where business cards get thrown around like confetti. But my introvert tendencies also mean that I can too easily give in to the temptation to cut myself off from the people who are like lifelines for my business and well-being.

We all need someone to listen to our ideas, reassure us that we're on the right path, and remind us that we have what it takes to succeed. By surrounding yourself with a network of supporters, advocates, and champions, you get to see your worth reflected back to you. Dealing with your inner critic is so much easier if you're surrounded by people who are rooting for you and want to help you succeed.

PRACTICE STRATEGIC GENEROSITY

You don't have to take on the world alone. Realizing your true potential starts with surrounding yourself with people who will challenge you, teach you, and open doors for you. And if you haven't found those people yet, have more conversations with people you admire. Ask them how you can support them. Give before asking for help.

When Marie Poulin joined me on the *Movement Makers* podcast, she described the buildup to releasing one of her signature programs. "For about two years before I launched, I was giving information away for free in Facebook groups. By the time I had something to offer other designers, they were already tagging me in Facebook groups and saying things like, *Oh, Marie might be able to help with that. She's the one to go to for this.* They remembered me as being really helpful. I call it Strategic Generosity."[74]

Strategic Generosity means giving through kindness without expectations but with the understanding that generosity will often pay you back.

Selena Soo described adopting a similar approach in her career as a publicity and marketing strategist on the podcast. "When you're coming from a place of giving, you're only contributing to someone's life in a good way," she explained. "A lot of people approach influencers from the standpoint of, *Oh my gosh, they're so amazing. What could they possibly need from me? They've got this amazing team. They've got this amazing audience. I'm going to be wasting their time.*"[75]

But Selena pointed out that if you approach people with that mindset, energetically, they will feel it and it will affect how they interact with you. "So the way that I found to level the playing field is by being someone who gives and contributes to their lives. Coming from that mindset helped me develop meaningful relationships with different influencers in my industry."

---

74   Nikki Groom, "Marie Poulin: Strategic Generosity and Tackling the Imposter Complex," *Movement Makers* podcast, accessed July 13, 2020.

75   Nikki Groom, "Selena Soo: Impacting Millions," *Movement Makers* podcast, accessed July 13, 2020.

Selena told the story of how she reached out to a well-known inspirational speaker and blogger and offered to help with her book launch by connecting her with some media people she knew. She got on the speaker's radar in that way, and now the individual's testimonial graces Selena's website, enthusiastically declaring, *"For the love of God, THANK YOU!"*

HERE ARE SOME MORE WAYS IN WHICH YOU, TOO, CAN PRACTICE STRATEGIC GENEROSITY:

- Invite someone you admire and want to add to your network for an interview, to speak at an event, or to co-host a webinar training so you can highlight their work and introduce them to more people.
- Spotlight them on your blog or on social media and be sure to tag them so they see it.
- Leave them a review for their book, podcast, or business online.
- Create an event featuring their book, take photos, and send to them afterward.
- Send them referrals whenever you come across someone who could use their services.
- Offer to become an affiliate for their program, product, or course.

You don't have to be an outgoing, charismatic influencer with hundreds of thousands of followers to benefit from a supportive community. When you make generosity part of your growth strategy, people will value your contributions and become avid supporters and champions.

WHO YOU NEED IN YOUR CORNER

Going after what we want in life is almost impossible if we try to do it alone. That's why it's vital to ensure we have supporters in our corner.

Those supporters might include:

Mentors who can give you the benefit of their experience and who are invested in helping talented women, like you, to get ahead. Mentors can either be people you get to know up close (for example, over coffee or a Zoom call), or you may learn from them from a distance (for example, through their podcast or YouTube channel). Mentors can be paid coaches—who can give you ongoing, dedicated, one-on-one support—or unpaid. For example, I coach a select number of women entrepreneurs one-on-one through my business and also offer free coaching for individuals through a local non-profit organization, which creates positive social and economic impacts by supporting social entrepreneurs and enterprises. If you can't yet afford a coach, look for non-profits in your area that provide opportunities for ongoing mentoring and support.

Sponsors who open doors for you, introduce you to people you need to know, and take responsibility for your success. They have reached a stage in their business or career where they have access to relatively more privilege and opportunities, and they want to share those with you as much as possible. Bear in mind that, although there's no standard set of steps to take to secure a sponsor, people generally want to invest in those who show promise and are willing to do the work. When you make new connections, don't be afraid to share your story and what you're passionate about. If people know you can help with a specific problem, you'll be the first person they call when that problem shows up on their radar. You can end up with a very symbiotic relationship in that way.

Strategic Partners are peers who believe in you and your work and who want to share their ideas and their network with you to help you succeed. You can form strategic partnerships by reaching out to people on social media or following up with people after you meet at an event and asking if they'd be open to connecting one on one. During your initial conversation, make a point of finding out about them and their goals for their business and ask them, "How can I support you?" Inevitably, they will ask you the same questions and ask if they can return the favor. Even if you don't have anything to promote when you first connect, keep a list of your strategic partners tucked away for when you need help with a project.

Champions are typically those people already in your corner—and they'll be there no matter what. They're your ride-or-die friends, your business besties, or your favorite coworkers who are open to conversations about whatever's on your mind. They have your back and you have theirs. You check in with one another regularly, and your conversations aren't only work related. Your champions are ideal for holding you accountable for any goals you set and will always be willing to put in a good word on your behalf. They believe in you, and they don't need any convincing to help you succeed.

Award-winning entrepreneur Kelsey Ramsden agrees that every successful person has a success pack behind them. "Top performers recognize that they're made up of the sum of their parts, which includes relationships. When you get into the hardest stuff, that's where the head game comes in and the people who succeed *do* and the people who don't succeed *don't* draw on the people around them."[76]

It took beating cancer for Kelsey to realize that she needed to reprioritize certain relationships. If you want to determine which of your relationships to prioritize, Kelsey recommends grabbing a piece of paper, putting a little "x" in the middle of it, and then drawing concentric circles around it, like a bullseye. After that, you can begin mapping all the people around you, like your partner, children, best friends, close relatives, friends from university, siblings, parents, trusted advisors, and colleagues: a smattering of the people around you and those you spend the most time with. The closest ones to you (the "x" in the middle) are the ones whose opinion you trust the most—what they say matters to you a great deal—while those on the outer perimeter are those whose opinions you trust the least.

Next, Kelsey said to list everyone's name on the other side of the paper in a chart and ask the following questions for each person:

- Do they support me personally?
- Do they support me professionally?
- Do they share great ideas?
- Do they provide useful information?

---

76 Nikki Groom, "Kelsey Ramsden: Surviving Success and Cancer," *Movement Makers* podcast, accessed July 13, 2020.

- Do they challenge me constructively?
- Do they inspire me?
- Do they anchor me?
- Do I have enough of a connection to that person that I would send them a card for a special occasion?
- Are they emotionally invested in me?
- Do I trust their opinion unequivocally?

Kelsey uses this exercise to help her better decide in which relationships to devote her time and energy. "It gives me a clear sense of [where] there are holes where I need to either find new relationships or develop the relationships I already have. When you disrespect those relationships, it's unlikely that they're going to serve you when you need them the most."[77]

🎧 **PODCAST TIP**

Listen to my interview with Kelsey Ramsden on the *Movement Makers* podcast when we talk about out how to develop the right relationships in the right way.[78]

Visit nikkigroom.com/category/podcast/.

COMMUNITY OVER COMPETITION

Not everyone necessarily values community. When I asked keynote speaker and author Kali Williams what she believes

---

77 Nikki Groom, "Kelsey Ramsden: Surviving Success and Cancer," *Movement Makers* podcast, updated July 9, 2018.

78 Ibid.

gets in the way of women fully stepping into their power, greatness, and potential, she agreed it's important that women support and uplift one another if we are to make the progress we want. "Women have often been obstacles for each other because of how the patriarchal system has taught us that we are in competition and that cattiness and backstabbing communication styles are the norm."

In Kali's book, *Ditch the Bitch Stigma: Embrace Your Inner Badass*, she refers to this as Queen of the Mountain Syndrome, where we are led to believe there is only one seat at the table—despite women being more naturally collaborative.[79] She explained to me that "when a woman gets to the mountain, she actually spends time kicking other women down off the mountain because she doesn't want to lose her hard-earned power. That, to me, is a huge problem, because rather than us banding together and truly becoming a unit of progression, we slap each other around metaphorically most of the time."

Kali experienced this herself when she decided to broaden her work as a sex educator to a mainstream audience. She discovered her peers had little interest in helping people like her climb because there was a sense—real or imagined—that there was a limited amount of money in the industry, and so others didn't want to share it by boosting younger voices. Experiencing some of those women being dismissive of her and treating her like she was a nobody was extremely disheartening for Kali. "It's a genuinely devastating feeling. It

---

79   Kali Williams, *Ditch the Bitch Stigma: Embrace Your Inner Badass*, Brazen Ink Press, October 31, 2019.

made me want to take revenge by being successful, like *I don't need you.*"

But while this type of treatment fueled Kali's fire, she pointed out that, ultimately, if we're not mentoring other women who come up after us or role modeling for them what's possible, "there is no future leadership."

In other words, our world is indisputably better when we decide to become more powerful in how we see ourselves *and* each other and use our collective strength to build a future that is worthy of all of us.

Kali explained that when a marginalized community truly believes they have the power and is no longer in-fighting, then it will much more likely to act as dynamite for the current systems, which reinforces the need for mentorship and sponsorship. "You need someone who's going to be in your corner, who's going to be fighting for you and alongside you."

I always say, "There's enough business for all of us," and I firmly believe that. We need to collectively work together to support one another rather than acting like it's our mountain top and there's only room for one of us at the peak.

When Jean joined the Movement Makers Mastermind, she was preoccupied with worrying about other entrepreneurs who were doing something similar to her. She felt threatened by them, and that competitiveness was taking her focus away from her goals.

I decided to level with her. "Jean, *no one* can show up in exactly the same way you do. You are uniquely qualified to do the work you do. No one can take that away from you. No one."

Jean left our call feeling much lighter, as though a weight had been lifted off her shoulders.

We don't need to one-up anyone else to get ahead. We don't need to feel threatened by what someone else is doing in our field—*especially* as women, because the odds are already stacked against us in so many ways.

It brings to mind a conversation my friend Patsy had with her coach, during which she was painting a vivid picture of riding a metaphorical wave she felt was about to crash over her head and leave her stranded on the shore at any moment.

"Whoa, hold up a minute," her coach interrupted, "You're not riding the wave. You *are* the wave."

I loved that reframe and have never forgotten it. We don't need to worry about competing with others because our work is unique to us and we're the only ones who can do it quite like we do.

* * *

As we reach the end of our journey together, I want you to know that not only do you have what it takes to succeed, but there are people in your corner who have your back, who want to help, and who understand the challenges you're up against.

Make it your mission to find those people.

USE THESE POWER PROMPTS
- Who's in *your* corner?
- Which supportive communities can you tap into that will help you succeed?

BORROW THIS POWER STATEMENT
May I remember that I'm not alone and that there are people who want to help me succeed.

WHAT'S NEXT?
I hope the stories and insights you've read in this book have inspired you and that you're turning these final pages with a better understanding of what it means to not only own your power, but also experiment with your purpose and continuously expand your vision of what's possible.

While our journey together might be coming to an end, there are plenty of ways for us to stay connected:

1. Start by visiting NikkiGroom.com to get access to resources including the **Movement Makers Community**, which makes openly available to members the kind of

insider information that has helped me and other business owners grow and make important decisions about our businesses. I've found that democratizing information in this way is a powerful way to empower entrepreneurs from all walks of life.

2. Post a review of this book on Amazon.com and on your blog or website.

3. Connect with me on social media @NikkiGroom (on Twitter, Instagram, Pinterest, and TikTok), or simply search "Nikki Groom" (Facebook and LinkedIn).

4. Share this book with someone you know who could use a boost, and tell them to come join us in the community too.

5. Check out the **Movement Makers Mastermind** and, if it looks like it could be a fit, apply for the next round today! Visit nikkigroom.lpages.co/mastermind-2020.

ACKNOWLEDGMENTS

I'm not sure what made me decide I wanted to be an author, but I do have an inkling *who* helped me arrive at that conclusion. Rita Bradshaw, you're proof that sometimes all a girl needs is her mum's best friend (who just so happens to be a bestselling author) to shine the way for her to follow. Thank you for inspiring me to put pen to paper.

Thank you to Jeff Daw, without whose encouragement I would still be talking about writing a book and not actually doing anything about it. Thank you for being a true champion throughout this entire journey. I am lucky to have a partner in life like you.

To Dave Ursillo, for the many months of coaching and support you provided me with as I began to explore the possibility of bringing this book to life. Thank you for helping me write the book I *wanted* to write, rather than the book I felt I *should* write.

To Eric Koester, our conversation couldn't have come at a better time. Thank you for your wisdom, your expertise, and the opportunity to experience your incredible book writing program. And to the entire team at New Degree Press—especially Brian Bies, Heather Gomez, Leila Summers, Michael Bailey, Cynthia Tucker, Kayla LeFevre, and Serhii Okomelhuk—I'm not sure I would have been brave enough to take the next step forward on my book publishing journey without your support, encouragement, and patience. Thank you for all that you do and continue to do.

To the incredible women I interviewed for this book, who entrusted me with their stories: Ashley Beaudin, Audrey Holst, Brandi Olson, Carrie Zarotney, Grace Quantock, Jennifer Brown, Kali Williams, Kim Sutton, Michelle Vitale, Tara McMullin, and many more—including those of you who participated in *The 100 Stories Worth Telling Project* or agreed to be interviewed on my podcast.

To all of those who supported my Indiegogo campaign and helped make this book a reality: Kathy Campbell, Anita Holt, Christine Meyer, Jennifer Berton, Jill Marinelli, Jane McAuliffe, Rob Beaven, Jennifer Brown, Rachel and Mark Wright, Brittanny Taylor, Scott Champagne, Jamie Bomback, Greg Faxon, Carrie Zarotney, Nichole Lewis, Jonathan Beck, Vicktoria Barokha, Laura Sorensen, Lauren Giammarco Silveira, Eric Koester, Doreen Ise, Jacqueline Smith, Zafira Rajan, Brian Panchuk, Cora Appleton, Kerry and Bobby Martin, Doug Foresta, Lynne Daw, Lindsey Daw, Jane Groom, Laura Groom, Debbie Jackson, Rene Harris, Anna Wood-Penn, Simony Resende, Janet Groom-Carroll, Christine and Terry Daw, Trudy Hall, Ali Fraenkel, Melissa Cord, Leah Goard, Cynthia Tang, Peter George, Talei Loloma, Bethany Warburton, Siân Harris, Amanda Krill, Michelle

Vitale, Amy Caracappa, Ali Willoughby, Winona Daw, Lisa Tamoua, Bethany O'Connor, Patsy Kenney, Sally Bozzuto, Srinivas Rao, Jo Saunders, Lisa Van Ahn, Sarah Robinson, Sarah Rainwater, Joanna Read, Kara Brunetta, Sharice Ennis, Lis Swain, Katie Mooney, Jeff Daw, Colleen Keable, Audrey Holst, Lucy Barr, Karen and Jennifer Bell, Shannon Wylie, and Esther Greenwood. I can't tell you how much joy it gives me to see all of your names in one place. Thank you so much for your early support.

To all of my incredible beta readers who took the time to read my first draft and provide feedback, I owe you big time! Anita Holt, Anna Woodpenn, Carrie Zarotney, Dave Ursillo, Geniece Brown, Karen Bell, Sarah Rainwater, Steve Disselhorst, Talei Loloma, and Winona Daw. A special mention goes to my amazing sister, Debbie Jackson, and my dear friend Cora Appleton—thank you both for going above and beyond! Your encouragement meant so much.

To Amelia Forczak, your insights and edits transformed my writing. I will forever be grateful to you for helping me bring my first Book Baby to life. I can't wait until we work together again!

To Jacquelyn Tierney, you absolutely knocked the cover design out of the park. Thank you for helping me look the part.

And last but not least, my family:

To Mum and Dad, thank you for always believing in me, always caring for me, and always being my biggest champions. I love you more than words can say.

APPENDIX

———

INTRODUCTION

Groom, Nikki. Movement Makers Mastermind. NikkiGroom.com. Accessed July 6, 2020. https://nikkigroom.lpages.co/mastermind-2020/.

CHAPTER ONE

"11 Facts About Teens and Self-Esteem." Do Something. Accessed July 10, 2020. https://www.dosomething.org/us/facts/11-facts-about-teens-and-self-esteem#fn5.

Allen, Amy. "Feminist Perspectives on Power." *The Stanford Encyclopedia of Philosophy*. Fall 2016 Edition. https://plato.stanford.edu/archives/fall2016/entries/feminist-power/.

"Brands in Action: Dove." Unilever USA. Accessed July 10, 2020. http://www.unileverusa.com/brands-in-action/detail/Dove-/298217/.

Brzezinski, Natalia. "Building Our Daughters' Self-Esteem, by Starting with Our Own." *HuffPost*. Updated November

2011. https://www.huffpost.com/entry/building-self-esteem-
buil_b_600860.

Fondiler, Ellen. "An Interview with Lisa Van Ahn." *Unlocked*.
Accessed June 24, 2020. http://ellenfondiler.com/an-interview-
with-lisa-van-ahn/.

"Get The Facts." National Organization for Women. Accessed July
10, 2020. https://now.org/now-foundation/love-your-body/
love-your-body-whats-it-all-about/get-the-facts/.

Harts, Minda. "Glass Ceilings Aren't Created Equal: Confronting
the Barriers Black Women Face in the Workplace." LinkedIn.
Published on September 13, 2019. https://www.linkedin.com/
pulse/glass-ceilings-arent-created-equal-confronting-barri-
ers-minda-harts/.

Jones, Kenneth and Okun, Tema. "The Characteristics of White
Supremacy Culture." From *Dismantling Racism: A Workbook
for Social Change Groups*. ChangeWork, 2001. Accessed July
13, 2020. https://www.showingupforracialjustice.org/white-su-
premacy-culture-characteristics.html.

Neuman, M.D., Fredric. "Low Self-Esteem." *Psychology Today*.
Posted April 14, 2013. https://www.psychologytoday.com/us/
blog/fighting-fear/201304/low-self-esteem.

Van Ahn, Lisa. "About I Am Girl." I Am Initiative. Accessed July
9, 2020. https://iaminitiative.com/about-i-am-girl/.

Van Ahn, Lisa. "About Lisa Van Ahn." I Am Initiative. Accessed
July 9, 2020. https://iaminitiative.com/about-lisa-van-ahn/.

CHAPTER TWO

Andrews, Nicola. "It's Not Imposter Syndrome: Resisting Self-Doubt as Normal for Library Workers." *In the Library with the Lead Pipe, an Open Access Peer Reviewed Journal.* Accessed on June 18, 2020. http://www.inthelibrarywiththeleadpipe. org/2020/its-not-imposter-syndrome/.

Casey, Jo. "Feminine Conditioning." JoCasey.com. Accessed on June 18, 2020. https://www.jocasey.com/feminine-condition-ing/.

Geisler, Tanya. "About." TanyaGeisler.com. Accessed on June 18, 2020. http://tanyageisler.com/about-contact#about.

Geisler, Tanya. "Diminishment and the Imposter Complex." TanyaGeisler.com. Accessed on June 18, 2020. http://tanyage-isler.com/blog/down-with-diminishment.

Goldhill, Olivia. "Is Imposter Syndrome a Sign of Greatness?" *QZ.* Accessed on June 18, 2020. https://qz.com/606727/is-imposter-syndrome-a-sign-of-greatness/.

Groom, Nikki. "Tanya Geisler: Stepping Into Your Starring Role." Accessed on July 8, 2020. https://nikkigroom.com/tanya-geis-ler-stepping-into-your-starring-role/.

Kay, Katty and Shipman, Claire. "The Confidence Code: The Science and Art of Self-Assurance: What Women Should Know." Harper Business. First edition, April 15, 2014.

Langford, Joe and Rose Clance, Pauline. "The Imposter Phe-nomenon: Recent Research Findings Regarding Dynamics,

Personality and Family Patterns and Their Implications for Treatment," *Psychotherapy* 30, no. 3, Fall 1993, Accessed on June 18, 2020. https://paulineroseclance.com/pdf/-Langford.pdf.

CHAPTER THREE

D'Simone, Sah. "Powerful Abundance Meditation - Manifest Your Dreams." Insight Timer. Accessed on July 13, 2020. https://insighttimer.com/sahdsimone/guided-meditations/powerful-abundance-meditation-manifest-your-dreams.

Hyatt, Michael. "Your Best Year Ever: A 5-Step Plan for Achieving Your Most Important Goals." Baker Books, 2018.

James, Matt, PhD. "4 Steps to Release 'Limiting Beliefs' Learned from Childhood." *Psychology Today.* Accessed June 19, 2020. https://www.psychologytoday.com/us/blog/focus-forgiveness/201311/4-steps-release-limiting-beliefs-learned-childhood.

Pearson O'Connor, Bethany. "Right on Time to Break the Cycle." *HuffPost.* Accessed June 19, 2020. https://www.huffpost.com/entry/lettin-it-shine_b_2908811.

Sophia Mohr, Tara. "Why Women Don't Apply for Jobs Unless They're 100 Percent Qualified." *Harvard Business Review.* Accessed July 6, 2020. https://hbr.org/2014/08/why-women-dont-apply-for-jobs-unless-theyre-100-qualified.

"The Five-Minute Journal: A Happier You in 5 Minutes a Day." Intelligent Change, 2013.

Quantock, Grace. "Using Your 'Brokenness' to Break Boundaries." TEDx Aylesbury. Accessed on June 19, 2020. https://www.youtube.com/watch?v=UN8_8q-KmdE.

CHAPTER FOUR

Feuerstein, George and Payne, Larry. *Yoga for Dummies*. For Dummies, 2014.

Groom, Nikki. "Diana Malerba: Brave-Hearted Survivor." *The 100 Stories Worth Telling Project*. Accessed July 13, 2020. https://nikkigroom.com/100storiesworthtelling-36-diana-malerba-brave-hearted-survivor/.

Groom, Nikki. "Gita Gavare Marotis." *The 100 Stories Worth Telling Project*. Accessed July 13, 2020. https://nikkigroom.com/gita-gavare-marotis/.

Groom, Nikki. "Tiffany Yu: Rebranding Disability Through the Power of Community." *The 100 Stories Worth Telling Project*. Accessed July 13, 2020. https://nikkigroom.com/100storiesworthtelling-47-tiffany-yu-rebranding-disability-through-the-power-of-community/.

Groom, Nikki. "The 100 Stories Worth Telling Project." NikkiGroom.com. Accessed June 20, 2020. https://nikkigroom.com/category/the-100storiesworthtelling-project/.

Volo, Karin. "1,352 Days: An Inspirational Journey from Jail to Joy." Life with a Fabulous View Incorporated, 2015.

CHAPTER FIVE

Brown, Brené. *The Gifts of Imperfection: Let Go of Who You Think You're Supposed to Be and Embrace Who You Are.* Hazelden Publishing, 2010.

Giordano, Simona. "Understanding the Emotion of Shame in Transgender Individuals – Some Insight from Kafka." *Life Sciences, Society and Policy.* Published October 2018. https://lsspjournal.biomedcentral.com/articles/10.1186/s40504-018-0085-y.

Groom, Nikki. "Brigitte Thériault: Cooking Her Way to a New Life." *The 100 Stories Worth Telling Project.* Accessed June 20, 2020. https://nikkigroom.com/story-worth-telling-11-brigitte-cooking-her-way-to-a-new-life/.

Groom, Nikki. "Elizabeth Cronise McLaughlin: Becoming a Powerful Force for Change." *Movement Makers* podcast. Accessed on June 20, 2020. https://nikkigroom.com/elizabeth-cronise-mclaughlin-becoming-powerful-force-change/.

Groom, Nikki. "Geniece Brown: No Shame in My Game." *The 100 Stories Worth Telling Project.* Accessed June 20, 2020. https://nikkigroom.com/geniece-brown-no-shame-game/.

Groom, Nikki. "Lindley Ashline: Discovering My Body Positivity." *The 100 Stories Worth Telling Project.* Accessed June 20, 2020. https://nikkigroom.com/lindley-ashline-discovering-my-body-positivity/.

Miller-Prieve, Vienna "Women, Shame, and Mental Health: A Systematic Review of Approaches in Psychotherapy." Retrieved from Sophia, the St. Catherine University repository website. Published May 2016. https://sophia.stkate.edu/cgi/viewcontent. cgi?article=1635&context=msw_papers.

Thériault, Brigitte. "How the Love of Food Saved My Life." *Daily Plate of Crazy*. Published January 2016. https://dailyplateof-crazy.com/2015/01/06/first-love-how-the-love-of-food-saved-by-life-by-brigitte-theriault/.

Thériault, Brigitte. "How to Use Your Story to Find Your Life Purpose." *Purpose Fairy*. Published October 2013. https://www.purposefairy.com/66478/how-to-use-your-story-to-find-your-life-purpose/.

CHAPTER SIX

Babauta, Leo. "Easier Decision-Making: Conduct Experiments." *Zen Habits*. Accessed June 21, 2020. https://zenhabits.net/test/.

Blake, Jenny. "Beautiful Questions for Challenging Times with Steve Morris." *Pivot Podcast*. Released March 29, 2020. http://www.pivotmethod.com/podcast/beautiful-questions.

Fields, Jonathan. *Uncertainty: Turning Fear and Doubt into Fuel for Brilliance*. Portfolio. Reprint edition, 2012.

Fields, Jonathan. "What if You Could Discover the Work You're Here to Do, Then Spend the Rest of Your Life Doing It?" Accessed June 21, 2020. https://www.goodlifeproject.com/sparketypes/.

Gilkey, Charlie. *The Small Business Lifecycle*. Jetlaunch, 2013.

Groom, Nikki. "Karin Volo: An Inspirational Story from Jail to Joy." *Movement Makers* podcast. Accessed July 13, 2020. https://nikkigroom.com/karin-volo-inspirational-journey-jail-joy/.

Poulin, Marie. "Are You Booking Your Clients Too Far in Advance?" MariePoulin.com. Accessed June 20, 2020. https://mariepoulin.com/blog/are-you-booking-your-clients-too-far-in-advance/.

CHAPTER SEVEN

Carroll, Leah. "The Founder of Girls Who Code Wants Women to Lose (and Win)." *Refinery 29.* Published March 6, 2019. https://www.bravenotperfect.com/refinery29/.

Carter, K. C. "KC Carter: Give Yourself Permission to Glow in the Dark." *Movement Makers* podcast. Accessed July 13, 2020. https://nikkigroom.com/kc-carter-give-permission-glow-dark/.

Faxon, Greg. "How to Pursue Your Goals (the Right Way)." GregFaxon.com. Accessed July 13, 2020. https://www.gregfaxon.com/blog/mantra.

Groom, Nikki. "Greg Faxon: Don't Let the Fear Win." *Movement Makers* podcast. Accessed July 13, 2020. https://nikkigroom.com/greg-faxon-dont-let-the-fear-win/.

Jarvis, Paul. "No One on the Internet Is Living the Life You Think They Are." Accessed on June 22, 2020. https://pjrvs.com/apples.

CHAPTER EIGHT

D'Ardenne, Kimberlee. "Invisible Labor Can Negatively Impact Well-Being in Mothers." Arizona State University website.

January 2019. https://asunow.asu.edu/20190122-discover-ies-asu-study-invisible-labor-can-negatively-impact-well-be-ing-mothers.

Elkins, Kathleen. "Self-Made Millionaires Agree on How Many Hours You Should Be Working to Succeed." Make It—CNBC. com. Published June 2017. https://www.cnbc.com/2017/06/15/self-made-millionaires-agree-on-how-many-hours-you-should-be-working.html.

Inc. Staff. "Why Startup Founders Need to Set Aside 18 Hours a Day for the First Year." *Inc.* Published November 25, 2015. https://www.inc.com/gary-vaynerchuk/askgaryvee-episode-90-18-hours-a-day.html.

McKeown, Greg. "Essentialism: The Disciplined Pursuit of Less." Currency, April 2014.

Schulte, Brigid. "Brigid Schulte: Why Time Is a Feminist Issue." *The Sydney Morning Herald.* Updated March 2015. https://www.smh.com.au/lifestyle/health-and-wellness/brigid-schulte-why-time-is-a-feminist-issue-20150309-13zimc.html.

US Bureau of Labor Statistics. "American Time Use Survey." Last modified December 2016. https://www.bls.gov/tus/charts/household.htm.

CHAPTER NINE
Groom, Nikki. "Kelsey Ramsden: Surviving Success and Cancer." *Movement Makers* podcast. Accessed July 13, 2020. https://nik-kigroom.com/kelsey-ramsden-surviving-success-and-cancer/.

Groom, Nikki. "Marie Poulin: Strategic Generosity and Tackling the Imposter Complex." *Movement Makers* podcast. Accessed July 13, 2020. https://nikkigroom.com/marie-poulin-strategic-generosity-tackling-imposter-complex/.

Groom, Nikki. "Selena Soo: Impacting Millions." *Movement Makers* podcast. Accessed July 13, 2020. https://nikkigroom.com/selena-soo-impacting-millions/.